The
Fax
Handbook

To my dad, Alexander A. Quinn

The
Fax
Handbook

Gerald V. Quinn

TAB **TAB BOOKS** Inc.
Blue Ridge Summit, PA

FIRST EDITION
FIRST PRINTING

Library of Congress Cataloging-in-Publication Data

Quinn, Gerald V.
   The Fax Handbook / by Gerald V. Quinn.
   p. cm.
   ISBN 0-8306-3341-3 (pbk)   ISBN 0-8306-4341-9
   1. Facsimile transmission. I. Title.
  TK6710.Q56   1989
  384.1′4—dc20   89-36600
                                                                                                    CIP

TAB BOOKS Inc. offers software for sale. For information and a catalog, please contact TAB Software Department, Blue Ridge Summit, PA 17294-0850.

Questions regarding the content of this book should be addressed to:

   Reader Inquiry Branch
   TAB BOOKS Inc.
   Blue Ridge Summit, PA 17294-0214

Acquisitions Editor: Kimberly Tabor
Technical Editor and Book Design: Lisa A. Doyle
Production: Katherine Brown

Illustrations by Gloria A. Ryan

Trademarks

Every effort has been made to supply trademark information about the company name, product, and services mentioned herein. Trademarks listed below were derived from various sources.

Fax Machines, Services, Supplies, and Accessories

AccuFax®	Papers Manufacturing Co.
Easy Link®	Western Union
Fax Care®	Fax Care Company
FaxPhone®	Canon U.S.A., Inc.
MagnaFax®	3M Company
MCI Mail®	MCI Telecommunications Corporation
NEC®	NEC Home Electronics
Panasonic®	Panasonic Company
Radio Shack®	Tandy Corporation
Telecopier®	Xerox Corporation

Computer and Computer Software Trademarks

Apple®, AppleFax®, and MultiFinder® — Apple Computer, Inc.

BackFax® — Solutions, Inc.

HP® — Hewlett Packard Corporation

IBM® and IBM PC® — International Business Machines Corporation

MacFax® — Orchid Technology

Macintosh™ — McIntosh Laboratory, Inc. Used with its express permission to Apple Computer, Inc.

MS DOS® — Microsoft Corporation

PageMaker® — Aldus Corporation

Thunderscan® — Thunderware, Inc.

Contents

Preface

SITTING IN MY FAVORITE CHAIR, I'M ENJOYING THE WARMTH COMing from the slow-burning fire in the fireplace. My thoughts are drowned by the comforts of the cozy living room. Light from the fire casts a warm glow about the room as I decide on a video to round out a comfortable evening at home. Suddenly from the study I hear a familiar sound—the phone rings and is answered by the familiar electronic handshake of two electronic devices communicating.

As I enter the study, a brief glance at the fax machine next to my desk tells me tonight won't be spent watching a video. Tonight will be spent in front of the computer editing the upcoming edition of a client's newsletter.

Just as my client's business continues to grow through enhanced communications via a customized newsletter to his customers, my client list is growing because owning a fax machine has enabled me to serve my customers better. Because I don't spend valuable time running across the state of New Jersey only to have clients check copy, I am more productive and able to beat the printers' deadlines. Although face-to-face meetings are still necessary, some intermediate steps are now just a few fax sessions. What was once a two-hour trip (round trip travel plus time spent waiting and meeting) is now just a few minutes of faxing back and forth plus a telephone conversation to communicate changes and/or ideas noted on the faxed documents.

Since most of my work is accomplished via the personal computer, I can send computer files to a printing service over the telephone via a computer modem and have the finished newsletter, brochure, article, etc. typeset and printed at the highest resolution without leaving home. The same printing service can send proof copies directly to me via the fax machine. Any corrections or modifications can then be indicated and faxed back to the printer before final copies are printed. It seems nearly impossible to calculate the time I now save thanks to my fax machine.

Time, Newsweek, Fortune—nearly every daily publication contains advertisements promoting the latest craze in office communications technology: the *facsimile* or "fax" machine. "Faxing" documents is becoming a standard means of communicating printed messages between two or more locations.

As of 1988, nearly 30 million people opted to commute to another room of the house rather than another city either full or part-time, and a third of all new businesses registered in 1988 operate out of the home. Many of these home-based businesses, such as my own, are possible due to the personal computer and related products: desktop publishing, personal copiers, fax machines, communication services, and other products of an information technology revolution.

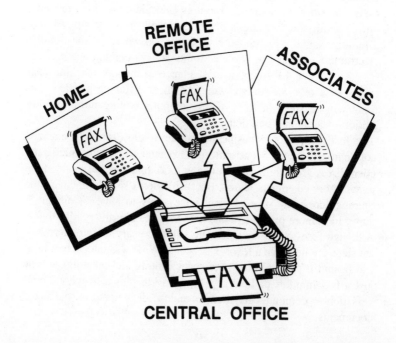

The advent of the affordable personal computer, capable of turning out sophisticated graphics as well as processing words and numbers, has been the driving force behind those working at home or in the small office environment. It is expected that by 1992, nearly one third of all U.S. households will own a personal computer. Coupled with improved and sophisticated telephone technology and information service organizations providing access to information on just about anything you can think of, the personal computer helped launch the Information Age. Now, the personal computer has the perfect complement—the personal fax machine. Together, the personal computer (or PC) and the personal fax machine enable the user to dig deeper and "byte" further into the Information Age.

The new darling in office technology is the fax. The facsimile machine offers expedition of message and document delivery. Is a fax machine in your future? Can a fax help you in your work? Answering yes to any of the following questions means that you're a candidate for a fax machine.

❖ Do you use overnight mail or other delivery services for correspondence?

❖ Do you need to send handwritten, drawn, or photographed materials to someone?

❖ Have you noticed a steady increase in your long-distance telephone charges?

❖ Do you work with information (reports, news items, press releases) that must be timely and/or is critical to your business?

❖ Do you receive information (contracts, reports, etc.) that must be rekeyed once it's in your office?

Whether you deal with information that is difficult to relay orally over the telephone such as schematics, drawings, designs, layouts, etc. or you just need to send a brief memo, you can communicate worldwide almost instantly at any time of the night or day via the fax.

The original fax machines, some of which cost more than $20,000, have been around for about 20 years. Fax machines are now available for under $1,000. These compact units fit on the edge of a desktop, connect to an ordinary telephone line, and are capable of sending a document in less than one minute.

Equally important is the emergence of the fax modem. Tying personal computers to fax machines and other PCs around the corner and around the world, the fax modem represents the marriage of the two most far-reaching revolutions in communications since the invention of television. Computers linked to fax machines and PC-fax networks become instant and automatic graphics communications systems. You can create a newsletter, for example, and send it to any place that has a PC-fax or stand-alone fax machine—all without ever touching a sheet of paper.

This book provides guidance in selecting, understanding, and using a fax machine. In addition, it describes the benefits of linking a personal computer to the power of fax. Although fax machines and PC-fax boards are sold under the premise that they are easy to use, effective use of them requires a knowledge of basic fax. From buying tips to maintenance hints, this book can help you understand the features and options available to the fax user. When your document absolutely positively has to be there, this book can help ensure it gets there.

Acknowledgments

A BOOK OF THIS NATURE IS POSSIBLE ONLY BECAUSE OF THE CO-operation, enthusiasm, and willingness of those in the fax industry to share their expertise and knowledge gained through years of experience and involvement in this exciting industry.

I thank those who met with me personally and through many telephone conversations and mountains of correspondence. Thanks to the many individuals who encouraged this publication and realize the need to inform and encourage the reader to pursue interests in this new technology.

Special thanks to those who extended their services and professional opinions to make this book possible: William Runyon and Gordon Clark of the Rowland Company, representing Canon U.S.A., Inc.; Peter Monninger of the Fax Care Company; Greg Snarski of Curtis Manufacturing Company, Inc.; AT&T; Radio Shack; James Sciales, representing Ricoh; Mindy Savar of Franklin Computer Corporation; Renee Mathews of Claris Corporation; Olduvai Corporation; Brian Smith of Thunderware, Inc.; Lauren Cammann of Solutions International; Judith Peterson, representing Quadram; James Thylin of Abaton; Alan Gillengerten of Electronic Speech Systems, Inc.; and the many other manufacturers who contributed photos and product information.

Deep appreciation is given to Gloria A. Ryan, who worked patiently to design, sketch, and then rework the diagrams and illustrations found in this text. Additionally, I am most appreciative for the assistance of Alex A. Quinn; Joan P. Diana, Head Librarian of Penn State University, Wilkes-Barre Campus; Norma H. Mc-Cormack, Historical Photograph Specialist at AT&T Archives; Gary C. Calderone; Joyce B. Cochrane; Frank A. Rito; William Donnelly; Anthony and Justin Brugnoli; and Dr. Michael Roth. And thanks to the many others from the communications industry who listened to my ideas and provided invaluable feedback that helped shape the direction and scope of this text in meeting the needs of the fax machine and personal computer/fax user.

Above all, thanks to my acquisitions editor, Kimberly Tabor, who helped make writing this text an exciting and rewarding experience through her assistance, encouragement, patience, and belief in this project.

Introduction

IN AN AGE WHEN TELEVISION CAN TAKE US TO THE SCENE OF major events happening throughout the world, it seems only natural that some power of instantaneous communications should filter down directly to the consumer. Television take us to the scene and radio lets us listen in, but the telephone puts us in direct contact with those important in our personal lives—from business associates to family and friends.

As AT&T has told us hundreds of times, "Reach out and touch someone." The electronic wonders of the Information Age enable even the most technologically unsophisticated consumer to reach out, tap, and gather data on almost any subject imaginable.

Our thirst for information has created a complementary response in the service and retail markets. Banks, for example, enable us to tap into our accounts through automated teller machines that provide ready access to cash regardless of the time of day or night. Overnight delivery services enable us to send a package and have it arrive at its destination by the next morning, guaranteed. And manufacturers have brought consumers more compact, powerful, and easy-to-use computers and computer software.

Those in the mainstream of the Information Age enjoy consuming mass quantities—mass quantities of reports, documents, stock quotes, newsletters, etc. It's a convenient pleasure to get responses to our questions, inquiries, and demands right off the shelf at the information supermarkets. Information supermarkets are arrays of diverse and specialized databases and information service bureaus. Most of these information bureaus require a subscription and the use of a computer and modem to tap into their various information warehouses.

Even the public library has expanded its role of meeting the information needs of patrons. Most libraries see their shelves expanding at a near alarming rate as the library tries to keep up with the information (magazines, reports, government documents, etc.) that patrons require and expect to find. To better meet demand, many public and private libraries now make extensive use of electronic document delivery services.

It is no surprise that the 20th century's oldest household communication device, the telephone, should play an ever increasing role in today's information rich and hungry society. From answering machines that keep track of our calls to sophisticated options such as caller ID, call waiting, call forwarding, etc., the telephone is indispensable to today's busy life-styles. The telephone has adapted well to change and has acquired many new skills.

The most important adaptation of the telephone to meeting today's information needs is possible because of tremendous improvements made in technology that the consumer never sees— improved communication links such as fiberoptic transmission lines, microwave transmission, and the electronic marvels of direct long-distance dialing. For example, improved telephone technology enables the personal computer user to plug a computer's modem into an ordinary telephone jack and communicate with other PCs, search through mountains of information, make travel arrangements, and order merchandise without ever leaving the room. (However, unlike PCs, which require considerable time to learn how to operate, fax machines offer nearly goof-proof operation.)

The PC-fax modem or PC-fax board represents the marriage of the fax machine and the personal computer. The PC-fax is expanding the world of instant communications even further. Connected to an ordinary telephone line and an RJ-11 telephone jack, the PC-fax connection brings the world of instantaneous "image communications" right to the desktop of even the most remote personal computer user.

Communication services and capabilities, once available to only the most technologically sophisticated corporations, are now accessible and readily available to those working at home, in the

small or corporate office, or visiting the local public library. This communication technology is now packaged in small lightweight units that occupy less space on the desktop than an ordinary type-writer.

Confronted by an array of models with all sorts of extra features, the consumer needs to carefully evaluate his/her fax needs. Some fax needs can be met easily by the stand-alone fax machine. Some will benefit most by the combination of a personal computer and appropriate PC-fax board. Still others might require the use of both machines.

In any event, fax machine and PC-fax board manufacturers as well as information service bureaus and organizations are well aware that, "can you fax that to me?" is fast becoming the hottest phrase in office communications language. It's also a phrase that warrants careful consideration before making any purchase decisions. Faxing documents is certainly something that most everyone wants to do. Consuming mass quantities is no longer a joke; it's quickly becoming a "fax" of life—both business and personal.

This book is designed to address the needs of the first-time fax buyer/user as well as those seeking to enhance and/or expand their present use of fax machines. The chapters can be read sequentially or independently of one another.

CHAPTER ONE

Fax Facts

TODAY "FAX IT TO ME" IS A PHRASE HEARD IN OFFICES THROUGH-out the world—from corporate headquarters to home-based business. Never before has the power of instantaneous communications been more important or used to such a degree as with today's fax transmissions. Everything from fast-breaking news to up-to-the-minute contract negotiations is being faxed—from around the corner to across the country to around the world. Paperwork, photos, drawings, and anything that can be communicated via a piece of paper can be sent and received at speeds of less than one minute per page rather than several days as required for a first-class letter sent coast-to-coast.

Improved technology and pared-down prices have currently made the fax machine the hottest-selling business accessory, and now the fax machine is even moving into consumers' homes. An ordinary telephone line, a thirst for information, and the need to "see it now" enable businesses and consumers alike to communicate with each other via the fax—all for the price of a phone call.

THE HISTORY OF FAX

Although the fax machine has made its way into offices and homes only recently, the idea and principle of fax transmission predates the integral part of today's fax communication—the telephone. The fax machine continues to teach us new uses for the telephone, from communicating between fax machines to communicating from a personal computer to an entire network of fax units.

Machines that operate similarly to today's fax, in principle, have been in use since the 1930s when they were first used to transmit weather maps. And news service organizations transmit photographs and accompanying stories to newspapers around the world using similar technology.

Where the Facsimile Got Its Name

It was the 17th Century Theologian Thomas Fuller who coined the term *facsimile*. It was he who first used facsimile in *The History of the Worthies of England*, applying the Latin phrase to the sort of writer we all know: "He, though a quick Scribe, is but a dull one, one who is good only at *fac simile*, to transcribe out of an original."*

Although the Latin phrase *fac simile* means to "make similar," the compressed phrase *facsimile* has meant "exact copy from transmission" since 1815. Today, the shortened term "fax" is used as a noun (short for fax machine), an adjective (fax machine or fax number), and a verb (to transmit or send a document—"fax it to me"). And now, in 1989, *The Oxford English Dictionary: Second Edition* contains the word *fax*.

The Origin of the Fax Machine

The fax machine is recognized for its ability to send documents back and forth almost immediately, saving time. Ironically, the electric clock spawned the invention of the fax.

In 1842, Alexander Bain, a Scottish inventor, developed an electrically controlled pendulum mechanism that enabled clocks to be synchronized in a master-slave arrangement. This meant that one clock could be set and control others interconnected in a timekeeping system.

Bain went on to develop a system that could send and receive a facsimile of dot patterns using the synchronized pendulum concept. In 1843 he received a British patent for an "automatic electrochemical recording telegraph." His device could print out a facsimile of dots on a sheet of electrosensitive paper.

---

*William Safire, "On language: Sit on my laptop," *The New York Times Sunday Magazine* (23 October 1988): 20.

Giovanni Caselli, an Italian expatriate, patented an improved version of Bain's invention. By 1865, France had the first commercial facsimile system connecting Paris with other cities in France. Other Frenchmen continued to make improvements upon Bain's original idea.

The predecessor to today's electronic image scanning systems was the "cylinder and screw" that was pioneered and demonstrated in 1850 by Englishman Frederick Bakewell. The cylinder or "drum" was in use until only recently.

Developments in fax technology remained slow with the next major advance occurring early in this century. A German, Dr. Arthur Korn, developed a system utilizing photoelectric scanning. It was Dr. Korn who, in 1902, successfully demonstrated the photoelectric fax system. This fax system could transmit and reproduce photographs. His system would link Berlin with London and Paris as early as 1910.

The first radio transmission of photographs between Europe and the United States occurred on June 11, 1922. Dr. Korn sent a photograph of Pope Pius XI from Rome to Bar Harbor, Maine.

Fax Developments in the United States

Commercial uses of early fax-related technology had taken place in the United States prior to Dr. Korn's trans-Atlantic transmissions. And during the 1870s, a system of start/stop synchronization was developed. (See "The Fax Handshake" in Chapter 2.) Near the end of the century there were developments in picture transmission.

Parallel to fax developments in Europe during the later 19th Century, in 1866 Professor Elisha Gray developed a system of electroharmonic telegraphy for the transmission of sounds over telegraph wires—the underlying technology for the development of the telephone. Nearby, Alexander Graham Bell labored to transmit the human voice by electric current on a wire. Both claimed credit for the invention at the United States Patent Office, but Gray had been three hours late.

The Gray National Telautograph Company, now OMNIFAX/ Telautograph Corporation and a leader in modern fax technology, was established in Virginia in 1888 after obtaining the patent for Gray's "telautograph." According to the original patent, the telautograph "enabled one to transmit his own handwriting to a distant point over a two-wire circuit."

While Gray's first telautograph was rather crude, a more sophisticated unit was developed during the following years. It was this "Standard" model that drew record crowds at the Chicago World's Fair in 1893.

Improvements culminating with the "Eureka" model of 1894 coincided with the first commercial installation of a telautograph in the offices of the American Bank Note Company. This achievement opened the doors for commercial acceptance of the telautograph as a valuable business communications tool.

Hotels were among the first users to take advantage of this early form of office automation. The ability of the telautograph to receive written messages while unattended was a revolutionary concept that adapted readily to many other businesses.

Throughout the 1920s and 1930s, telautographs could be found in virtually every form of private enterprise and public service. Hence, America was getting used to fax documents as early as the 1920s.

Fax Meets the Press

The year 1924 was a historic one for picture transmission systems in the United States. AT&T (American Telephone and Telegraph), RCA, and Western Union each demonstrated their own systems that same year. In May of 1924, AT&T was the first to demonstrate the remarkable achievement of transmitting a 5-by-5-inch picture from Cleveland to New York—over 500 miles—in only four and one-half minutes. That July, RCA successfully transmitted a photo across the Atlantic Ocean to England and back again. Western Union inaugurated its short-lived "Telepix." AT&T placed its commercial picture transmission system in service in 1925, and RCA's radiophoto network debuted in 1926.

During the later 1920s, Western Union searched for a way to use facsimile transmission to broaden its telegraph message service. This search led to the nonelectrolytic direct recording paper and the firm's automatic facsimile telegraph system which was popular during the 1930s and 1940s. In 1948, Western Union introduced the *Desk-Fax*, a desktop fax message transmitter. Western Union had nearly 50,000 in operation.

Beginning in 1930, the fax saw its use expand from news picture transmission to include the regular transmission weather data. RCA began the radiofacsimile transmission of weather maps to ships at sea in 1930. Today, weather maps are still faxed to ships around the world.

PICTURE TRANSMITTED OVER TELEPHONE LINES

BY THE

AMERICAN
TELEPHONE AND TELEGRAPH
COMPANY

ORIGINAL PHOTOGRAPH

PHOTOGRAPH AS RECEIVED OVER TELEPHONE LINES
Simultaneously at New York, Chicago and San Francisco

PHOTOGRAPH OF NEWSPAPER REPRODUCTION OF
TRANSMITTED PICTURE
As It Appeared in the *New York Sun*

☏ *AT&T was the first to transmit the* newspicture *(1925). Original picture (top) was transmitted from Washington, D.C., received simultaneously in New York, Chicago, and San Francisco (center), and published in the* New York Sun, *Wednesday, March 4, 1925. (Courtesy of AT&T Archives)*

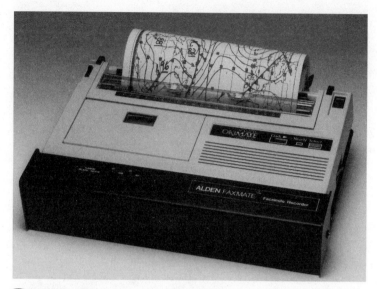

☎ *The Alden Faxmate is a complete marine information station that receives weather charts (Weatherfax), Radioteleprinter, and Navtex messages. (Courtesy of Alden Electronics, Westboro, MA)*

In 1934, The Associated Press took over operation of AT&T's picture transmission system. The Associated Press named its newly acquired service, "Wirephoto." The power and flexibility of this service caused others to create similar news picture networks.

Until the 1950s, Acme, Times Telephoto Equipment (renamed Times Facsimile), Finch Telecommunications, RCA, Western Union, and Radio Inventions, Inc. were the leading manufacturers of fax machines. The Bell System (Bell Labs and Western Electric Company) stopped production of fax units. Bell's parent company, AT&T is a major contender in today's fax market.

Fax Newspapers

In 1926, Austin Cooley was broadcasting news stories via his "Ray Photo" system. His company, Times Facsimile, later became a dominant force in the facsimile machine market. Cooley believed the fax machine could become a household appliance.

While Cooley was developing his system, Austrian Captain Otho Fulton's "Fultograph" went into operation. Fulton's system could broadcast pages about the size of a postcard. Images were recorded on special electrolytic paper.

In 1929, General Electric demonstrated a radio facsimile that could print images using carbon paper for impact printing on plain paper. Later, RCA built machines based on the carbon paper concept and used them for home demonstration purposes.

John Hogan invented the "Radio Pen" and in 1934 successfully demonstrated this fax broadcast method with the cooperation of radio station WTMJ in Milwaukee. Hogan's system used an ink stylus to record transmissions on paper. Unfortunately for Hogan, the "Radio Pen" had little impact on the market and soon faded into history.

Convinced that radio transmission of newspapers would be an important marketing triumph, the St. Paul, Minnesota Radio Station KSTP broadcast a special edition newspaper by radio facsimile in 1937. One of several stations to follow the St. Paul station, W2XBF of New York City became the first station to be granted an FCC experimental facsimile broadcasting license. The New York station was owned and operated by W.G.H. Finch, a major fax manufacturer.

By the late 1930s, the Federal Communications Commission, having recognized the importance of fax broadcasting, required that a minimum of 50 homes within a fax broadcast area be equipped with fax receivers. With more than 1,000 fax receivers located throughout the country, complete radio-dispatched newspapers could be broadcast throughout the night and read by families the following day.

Having captured the attention of radio buffs, approximately 40 radio stations were regularly broadcasting fax newspapers by 1941. Beginning in the mid 1940s, the Miami Herald, the Philadelphia Inquirer, the New York Times, and the Chicago Tribune began to broadcast special fax edition newspapers via FM. On June 9, 1948, the FCC granted official fax broadcasting licenses.

TV Pulls the Plug on Fax

Interest in fax newspaper broadcasting had generated considerable excitement, but the advent of television would pull the plug on the idea of a fax newspaper machine in every home. Television could now bring news and world events into the home in such a way that even movie theaters would suffer from empty seats as audiences chose to stay home and watch TV.

And so, the fax machine would remain quietly sending and receiving pictures and news behind the scenes at newspapers and transmitting important documents for major corporations. In addition, the market for special application fax machines, such as those for marine purposes, would keep many fax manufacturers busy.

THE REBIRTH OF THE FAX

The advent of a nationwide dial telephone network in the 1960s saw a renewed interest in fax machines. No longer dependent on individual operator assistance, companies now saw the fax machine as an important business tool. Magnavox was the first company to offer the desktop, telephone-coupled (acoustic coupler) fax machine: the Magnafax 840. The Magnafax was later licensed to Xerox and marketed as one of the Xerox Telecopiers. Later Xerox manufactured its own line with Magnavox continuing to market its Magnafax line. These machines were joined by others from manufacturers such as Stewart-Warner and Graphic Sciences, Inc.

Commonly referred to as Group I fax machines, the fax machines of the 1960s were analog units capable of transmitting a page within four to six minutes. These acoustic-coupled machines required the user to place the handset of the telephone into a special cradle. Analog signals from the sending fax were then broadcast via ordinary telephone lines to a receiving fax.

In 1972, Magnavox sold its product line to 3M which had been marketing a Japanese-manufactured fax machine. Japanese manufacturers would soon lead the way in marketing affordable fax machines with sophisticated features and functions.

The mid seventies saw additional companies jump into the fax marketplace. Panafax, part of the Matsushita Corporation, was one giant to enter the fax race. Harris Corporation was another.

Group II fax machines debuted in the mid seventies. Capable of transmitting a page within two to three minutes, these machines were developed in the United States by Graphic Sciences (since absorbed by Fujitsu) and 3M.

TODAY'S FAX—30 SECONDS OR LESS

The Japanese would demonstrate their ability to improve upon existing technology by creating still another family or group of fax machines—the faster, more powerful Group III fax machines. Developed in the mid seventies, these machines comprise nearly all of the fax units sold today. Transmitting at about 9 to 20 seconds per page, these digital units offer a range of capabilities that can increase productivity while reducing operating costs.

Group III machines can operate as stand-alone units or as part of a network. Although digital, they can switch to analog mode to communicate with older Group II and Group I machines. Memory and automated functions enable these machines to operate unattended, any time of the day or night.

Statement of Fax

The continuing growth of the fax market is fueled in part by the standards that govern its manufacture. Regardless of manufacturer, almost every fax manufactured today can communicate with fax machines from any other manufacturer. Even the sophisticated digital fax can communicate with some older Group I and Group II fax machines and vice versa. Group III standards were established

☎ *Canon's Fax-270, with its Ultra High Quality (UHQ) digital processing, sets a new standard in facsimile image reproduction. (Courtesy of Canon U.S.A., Inc.)*

in 1980 by the CCITT (Consultative Committee on International Telephone and Telegraph). CCITT standards classify the stages of fax technology and establish their compatibility and communication protocols.

Today, the fax is the predominant means by which documents (text and graphics) are exchanged electronically between two points. Any document that can be sent by mail (electronic or E-mail) or ground (United States Postal Service or Overnight Mail Services) can be faithfully reproduced via a fax machine. Whether the stand-alone fax machine or one of the new PC-fax boards is used to transmit documents, fax remains the most readily available, flexible, and cost-effective method by which to communicate— whether you need to fax to a place around the corner or around the world.

Tomorrow's Fax: Today

The fastest fax to date is the Group IV fax. Fax units in this group offer the highest resolution (up to 200 dots, or pixels, per inch at a transmission rate of just five seconds). However, Group IV machines require access to digital telephone lines, which won't be widely available until the 1990s.

In the meantime, Group III machines continue to dominate the fax market with new applications occurring almost daily. New features, improved operation, and dramatically lower prices (especially low-end entry models) will undoubtedly help the fax machine become as common as the VCR. "Do you have a fax machine?" will undoubtedly be replaced with, "What's your fax number" or "will you fax it to me?"

The latest fax machines don't require a dedicated phone line. Some units don't require manual switching to fax mode because they can differentiate between a voice phone call and another fax unit. Group III machines will undoubtedly retain their foothold in the market until well into the 1990s, particularly with the home and small-office market. Group V and VI machines are on the drawing boards.

The development of the fax machine has taken many steps, especially within the past ten years. Improved technology coupled with the miniaturization of circuitry has given today's compact fax units capabilities that giant corporate fax machines did not have five years ago. The next chapter examines the principles behind how the fax works.

CHAPTER TWO

How It Works

DOCUMENTS OF ALL KINDS—ARTICLES, CONTRACTS, PHOTOS, drawings, or anything that can be communicated via a piece of paper—are now sent and received across the United States in as little as 15 seconds instead of several days as required for a first-class letter sent coast to coast.

The facsimile market is exploding. Improved technology and lower prices have made the fax machine the hottest selling business accessory, and now fax machines are racing into consumers' homes. An ordinary telephone line, a thirst for information and the need to "see it now" enable businesses and consumers alike to communicate with each other via the fax. Fax is perceived as convenient and unobtrusive—it's there when you need it and you don't even have to leave the room to send and receive important information.

The fax machine's ease of use and dependable operation have fueled its growth. In many ways, the fax machine is a model of efficiency and utility—an ideal appliance for office and home. But how does it work?

HOW DOES MY FAX TALK TO OTHER FAX MACHINES?

The magic of fax is that the consumer needn't know much about how the machines operate. However, the consumer does need

☎ *Whether it's from around the corner or around the world, a fax machine can help make communications more timely and effective anywhere there's a phone.*

to understand the vast array of features found on fax machines. The features manufacturers build into their machines make faxing economical, goof-proof, and reliable.

A fax machine sends or transmits a hard copy of text, pictures, etc., over an ordinary telephone line to another remote fax machine. Using a digital process to scan and encode what is fed into the machine, the fax then converts digital information to analog form so that information can then be sent over the telephone line. The receiving fax decodes the analog signal, converts it back into a digital format and prints out on thermal-sensitive paper as each line is received.

Compact Electronics

Today's fax machines make extensive use of large-scale integration (LSI) circuits to replace a multitude of individual electronic components. LEDs (light-emitting diodes) and CCDs (charge-coupled devices) are used in the scanning mechanisms. LSI circuits give fax machines their digital capabilities to communicate with all other fax machines.

CCDs and LEDs virtually eliminate the need for moving parts in the scanning mechanism. CCDs, LEDs, and LSI circuitry are responsible for the speed at which documents are scanned and perform feats such as compressing white space. (Fax machines compress data by ignoring white space in documents and moving quickly to areas of the document with text, line drawings, shading or photos.)

Data compression in the form of redundancy reduction or skipping white space enables fax machines to communicate at fast speeds, sending a page of text in as little as 12 seconds. The scanning device is the "eyes" of the fax machine.

How a Fax Sees

Fax machines work much like standard office photocopiers. Printed material (photos, text, etc.,) is fed into a scanning device that scans each line, and electronic circuits convert it into corresponding electronic signals capable of being transmitted over standard phone lines. The receiving fax unit converts the signals and prints the corresponding image or facsimile on thermal paper. (High-end fax machines utilize laser printers—as do personal computers tied to fax machines.)

Reproduction quality depends on the resolution of the scanner or how well the scanner can break down the scanned image into tiny dots or *pixels* (the light and dark picture elements that make up the image). The number of dots comprising a newspaper photo is a good example. Resolution is rated in lines per inch (or dots per inch) scanned horizontally and vertically.

The standards for scanning and image transmissions have been set by the CCITT (Consultative Committee for International Telephone and Telegraphy) Facsimile Committee. Group III fax machines conform to established standards that enable them to communicate with each other and deliver resolutions of 200 LPI horizontally and 100 or 200 LPI vertically. Some fax machines have a fine mode with even higher resolution; however, the higher the resolution, the longer the communication process takes.

Fax machines operate in one of two ways:

❖ CCD (charge-coupled device)—A sheet of paper is guided into the fax unit where a CCD (charge-coupled device) image pickup scans the document line by line. In order for scanning to take place, the paper is flooded with a bright light as it passes through the machine. An array of mirrors bounces the image into a lens where it is read by the CCD. The CCD in the fax machine operates similarly to the CCD image pickup found in camcorders and video cameras.

❖ CIS (contact image scanning)—This method, found on somewhat pricier fax machines, uses an array of LEDs to scan a sheet of paper as it passes through the machine. The document passes through a strip of LEDs. The reflected light from each LED is captured by a special image receptor via a fiberoptic link. The machine records an "on" signal for a dark spot and an "off" signal for white paper. Special sensing circuits encode image information into analog (audible) form for transmission over the telephone line. The receiving fax machine translates the analog information into on/off signals or dot/no-dot (pixels) instructions for its built-in printer to print the facsimile of the image transmitted by the sending fax machine.

Fax transmissions differ from ordinary computer modem transmissions in that everything seen by the scanner (drawings, text, even signatures) comes through. The process is similar to using a photocopier, but the copy (facsimile) appears at the receiving fax unit. Machines have varying gray scale capabilities with numbers ranging from 16 to 64 shades of gray.

The Steps of a Fax Transmission

Step 1. A document is fed into the fax machine where a scanner creates an electronic representation of the document by describing the image according to the "blackness" of each dot or pixel on the page. The scanning is a raster pattern (left to right and top to bottom). A pixel that is either black or white (not gray) is referred to as a *pel*.

Group III fax machines have an average resolution of 200 pels/inch. As explained above, the scanner sees each dot as either black or white. Digitally, that means each black dot is a "1" and each white dot is a "0." Each 8.5-by-11-inch page is comprised of 3.7 million pels and takes 3.7 million bits to describe one page—an amazing feat by any measure.

Step 2. The number of bits required to describe the image (a single page) is reduced by a special processor. The compressed electronic representation of the image is achieved by describing the boundaries of the black pels. Most (more than 50 percent) of the pels comprising the average page are white; therefore, fewer bits are needed to describe the page.

Step 3. A modulator converts the bit sequence (1s and 0s) to an analog signal so that the telephone lines can carry the image information.

Step 4. A receiving fax machine is called either manually or automatically at an appointed time, and the modulated signal is sent to the remote fax unit.

Step 5. The receiving fax machine demodulates the analog telephone signals back into digital code, which restores the compressed electronic representation of the image.

Step 6. A decompressor restores the electronic representation or bit map of the image.

Step 7. A bit map (facsimile) is printed out on a sheet of thermal paper or via a laser printer on high-end fax machines. Most fax machines print on thermal paper. This paper is chemically treated to darken in response to heat beyond normal storage temperatures. A resistive element capable of rapid temperature changes responds to varying current, causing an image to appear as the paper passes over it. (Note: Thermal paper left on the dash of a car in hot weather will quickly turn completely black.)

The Fax Handshake

Transmitting to a remote fax machine requires that both sending and receiving units operate together. Whenever a fax machine answers a call, you will hear a distinctive sound. This sound enables the machines to establish a connection (handshake). The first part of the connection is the *phasing*. Phasing positions the scan and recording or printing mechanisms so that they coincide with respect to their relative positions. (As the sending machine scans, the receiving machine is printing.) The second part of fax communication is *synchronizing*, or keeping the phase (start/stop) synchronized (in step with each other) so one machine doesn't get ahead of the other.

FAX GROUPS

The CCITT has defined four distinctive fax groups. Each group has defined standards for transmission quality (resolution) and speed.

Group I. Machines in the Group I class send the modulated, simple electronic representation as a pixel map with about seven shades of gray and a resolution of 96 pixels per inch. These machines were introduced in 1966 and took six minutes to send a single 8.5-by-11-inch page.

Group II. Introduced in the mid seventies, these machines used compression modulation to double transmission speed to approximately 3 minutes per page. Gray-scale abilities were dropped from the machines. Group II units were common in many larger businesses and are quickly giving way to more cost-effective Group III units.

Group III. The increased speed of these machines gave fax its big push into the marketplace. Introduced in 1974, these digital units were standardized in 1980 by the CCITT. Improved compression (bit code and white space) coupled with a digital modem and an automatic system to ensure accurate transmission, Group III units can send a full page of text in as little as 20 seconds.

These digital units are extremely cost effective to use because of reduced transmission time. They can operate unattended when telephone rates are the lowest and can communicate with PCs via a fax modem/board. Most Group III fax units can transmit from 16 up to 64 shades of gray. These machines will continue to hold the lion's share of the small business/home fax market well into the 1990s when Group IV units will dominate the high-end business market.

Group IV. Standards for these units were developed between 1980 and 1984. Omitting the modem, Group IV units transmit to computer networks via Public Data Networks (PDN). Sophisticated error checking ensures error-free transmission. Since the data is delivered as a continuous stream, printing is done after the transmission, unlike Group III units which print each line as it is received (phase and synchronization).

Group IV units are considered high-end machines capable of high resolution and can be tied to scanners, OCR (optical character recognition) devices, and laser printers. The sophistication and expanded capabilities of Group IV units has led to three classes of Group IV units, depending on the functions used.

❖ *Class 1*. This class of Group IV fax units is compatible with Group III. Group IV units must produce a minimum resolution of 200 pels/inch or the Fine Mode (highest resolution) of Group III.

❖ *Class 2*. Units in this class operate at a resolution of 300 pels/inch. They also require internally stored characters and fonts and protocols that enable them to communicate with European Teletext.

❖ *Class 3*. These fax units can scan an image and text via an OCR and actually recognize fonts, therefore enabling the unit to send text in a manner similar to communicating with a word pro-

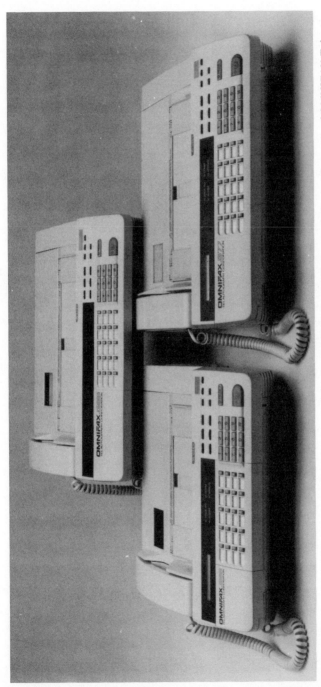

☎ *Three high-speed facsimile models available from century-old OMNI-FAX/Telautograph Corp. (Courtesy of OMNIFAX/Telautograph Corp.)*

cessor. Class 3 must also be able to transmit to Teletext. The highest resolution is 400 pels/inch.

Group IV units require special digital telephone lines that won't be widely available until the mid nineties. Group III units are the dominant force in today's fax communications and will remain so into the late nineties, especially with the consumer. Therefore, consumers can feel assured that a Group III fax unit will remain current for at least 10 years—CCITT standards have ensured that.

Fallback and Noise

A feature common to Group III fax machines is automatic fallback. *Fallback* occurs when a Group III machine fails to connect to another Group III at the fastest transmission rate. When transmission difficulty occurs, these units automatically fall back or drop down to a slower transmission speed, for example, from 9,600 bps to 7,200 bps, 4,800 bps, or 2,400 bps as needed. Interference such as lightning, power line noise, and poor quality phone lines can cause transmission difficulties. Group III machines adjust transmission rates to keep units in phase and synchronized. Should line difficulties prevent transmission, most machines will flash a "line fail" notice. (Note: Most Group III machines can adjust transmission speeds when communicating with an older Group II or I unit.)

Group III is Here to Stay

Manufacturers have developed features and options that enable Group III fax machines to make optimum use of telephone transmission capabilities. From unattended operation during off-peak hours to broadcast capabilities, today's fax machines maximize telephone line capabilities. A Group III fax is, without question, the unit for the small business/home user. The fax machine buyer's task is to identify his/her fax needs and find the machine that can meet those needs—from "low-end" or basic fax to advanced feature-laden units.

CHAPTER THREE

The Fax Advantage

THE NEED TO COMMUNICATE "NOW" HAS LED TO THE PHRASE "Fax it to me" and is heard in offices and homes across the country. No longer content to get it overnight, let alone several days later via the postal system, Americans are beginning to depend on the fax. From busy executives who travel extensively and find the fax an easy way to transmit and receive important business documents to friends exchanging an interesting magazine article, the fax machine has come a long way since the Scottish clockmaker, Alexander Bain, invented the first fax in 1842 (See Chapter One).

Bain's invention could transfer an image from one sheet of electrically conductive paper to another via an electric wire. And today, nearly 150 years later, the modern fax machine transfers images from a sheet of paper to a sheet of thermal paper via telephone wires. Although the concept is the same—getting information from one location to another in hard copy—present-day fax units are able to communicate with each other as well as with personal computers (and vice versa).

Modern technology has given fax machines increased transmission speeds coupled with all kinds of dazzling features that can confuse even the seasoned fax user. The true advantage of "faxing a document" is not found in the smart looks of the personal fax unit, but rather in the cost-effective communications made possible by these compact units.

Before purchase decisions are made, the potential fax buyer needs to examine how the use of a fax can improve communications and lower the rising costs of using traditional, overnight, and E-mail (electronic mail) document delivery services. In a relatively short time, the use of a fax machine can save more than the cost of the unit by way of improved speed in correspondence that could lead to an increase in business volume.

WHAT CAN FAX DO FOR YOUR BOTTOM LINE?

A fax can reduce expenses, increase profits, and save time by providing fast, accurate, and cost-effective communication. A few of the ways fax can help your business and/or personal communications are:

❖ A fax machine can send correspondence/documents to remote fax locations at the touch of a button, even when unattended.

❖ A fax machine can help you meet time-sensitive deadlines.

❖ Since fax transmissions are accurate with highly legible reproduction, clients get to see items (proposals, layout plans, etc.) as they are discussed over the phone.

❖ Fax makes frequent updates and revisions easy and up-to-the-minute.

❖ Fax makes it easy to share information already on paper (e.g., memos, letters or forms) and eliminates errors caused by verbal communications.

❖ Unlike telex, fax requires no special training or special skills, reducing clerical time.

❖ Fax makes communication of text, graphics, and photos between branch offices and remote locations easy.

❖ Fax eliminates the delay in getting important documents seen and approved.

❖ Fax makes business more competitive by providing a means to get price quotes, bids, and confirmation of orders as quickly as dialing the telephone.

❖ Time-saving features found on many fax units enable these machines to communicate at off-peak hours when phone rates are lowest.

❖ Many units ensure confidentiality of faxed documents through built-in security and/or privacy features.

❖ Some fax machines are multifunctional, operating as a combination telephone, fax machine, copy machine, and answering machine.

No Justifiable Alternatives to Fax

There are alternatives to speedy document delivery: courier services, telex, E-mail (electronic-mail), and the postal service. However, fax has the cost advantage. Any business that relies on speedy exchange of information, particularly text or graphics, will have a difficult time trying to justify not having fax service. The question that soon emerges is, "Why hold up business by waiting hours or days for delivery of information when fax enables information to be shared in seconds?"

Instead of using fax services, the occasional fax user might find owning a fax machine is justified due to dramatic price reductions on basic models. And for those individuals, a basic model with limited features should prove more than adequate.

Many individuals and small businesses underestimate the volume of fax they will send and buy a "low-end" fax. Suddenly they find themselves in need of a fax machine with enhanced features such as broadcast capabilities and a multipage document feeder. And, it is important to consider the probability of an increase in the volume of faxed material, both sending and receiving. Therefore, don't buy a machine that meets your minimum requirements. Plan for an increase in fax use and buy accordingly.

☎ *Canon's affordable FaxPhone 15 combines advanced telephone and facsimile features in a compact, lightweight design that's ideal for corporate and home office use. (Courtesy of Canon U.S.A., Inc.)*

IMPORTANT CONSIDERATIONS

Before rushing out to buy or lease a fax machine, consider the following points. The assumption should be that fax is here to stay, and you want to gain the enhanced communications made possible by fax.

Q. Will you send and/or receive more than five pages at a time (including cover page)?

A. Yes means you might want a machine with an automatic paper cutter that can fax more than five pages unattended. The paper cutter makes it easy to deal with the reception of long documents—try cutting apart 15-page transmissions several times a day. The larger capacity feeding mechanism avoids time wasted manually feeding individual sheets of paper into the fax. In addition, make sure the fax can handle the size of paper you normally use for your work. Most machines accept an input document up to 8.5 inches wide. Document length is generally no problem except for the possible limitation of the length of the paper roll for printing. Check on the maximum length of the paper supply for printing. Individual needs might dictate a fax machine with a large roll capacity.

Q. Do you anticipate sending more than 10 pages per day?

A. Yes means you probably need a machine that can send documents both unattended (*auto dialing*) and at predetermined times when telephone rates are lowest (*delayed transmission*).

Q. Will you be sending the same document to more than one location?

A. Yes means you should consider *broadcast* features that enable you to send the same documents to multiple locations.

Q. Do you need to send or receive daily reports to or from a central location?

A. If so, *polling* is a feature that enables one fax machine to call another and request a document. You merely place the document to be faxed in the fax machine. When the other fax calls, the document will be sent automatically. Machines that poll back and forth utilize an identification code that is set the same for each machine. The security code ensures that only authorized users receive the information.

Q. Do you sometimes send sensitive information?

A. If so, you should consider machines with *confidential transmission* capabilities.

Q. Do you anticipate receiving and sending documents many times throughout the day?

A. Transmissions sent and received during the day can tie up important phone lines and make it difficult for customers/clients to reach you. You should consider a dedicated telephone line for the fax machine unless most transmissions will take place after business hours. Many phone companies offer reduced rates for telephone lines used for fax machines.

Q. Do you know where you want to place the fax machine?

A. Accessibility to the fax machine is very important, but not at the expense of others. Those sitting near a busy fax machine soon find the noise annoying. Placement in a mutually agreeable location is of the utmost importance. In addition, a fax machine requires access to an electric outlet and telephone jack.

Q. Does the dealer have trained sales persons who specialize in fax machines?

A. Most discount outlets and catalogue stores have sales personnel who are inexperienced with fax machines. Besides being familiar with the fax machine, knowledgeable sales personnel should understand the fax needs of both the small business and the individual consumer. A good price does not necessarily mean a fair price.

Q. Do you know where to obtain service for a fax machine?
A. Fax machines are very dependable, but they might need occasional servicing as with any machine. Most office supply stores provide in-store service. If not, before deciding upon a particular brand of fax machine, identify those manufacturers with the most conveniently located service facilities. Some fax machine manufacturers offer toll-free, on-line diagnostics that can often correct fax transmission difficulties right over the phone.

FAX NEEDS CHART

The purchaser of a fax machine for a rapidly growing business, or one that deals with mail order, might find a fax is an absolute necessity. However, for those who must see the effect a fax might have on the "bottom line," the chart on page 25 will help calculate the cost benefits of a fax.

To calculate the cost benefits of faxing, first record the cost whenever you send a document via messenger service or express mail. Next, call the receiving party and see if they have a fax machine. If they have a fax machine, you could be sending documents instantly and at a fraction of the cost. If you call a particular party on a regular basis, call your long distance telephone service and they will tell you the exact cost to call that number. The cost benefits of faxing a document can be very surprising.

THE SELF-GENERATING FAX

Fax is a self-generating technology. The more fax machines find their way into offices and homes, the more useful fax becomes. From public libraries using fax to receive information requests and sending responses to patrons, to corner delicatessens accepting faxed orders, fax is becoming an accepted way of communicating. The question is no longer, "Do we need a fax?" but rather, "What kind of fax machine do we need?"

Chapter Four examines the features found on current fax machines and how those features can help you get the max from a fax.

Cost–Benefits Comparision Chart Fax vs Overnight Services				
Express Mail, Overnight, etc.			**Long–distance connect charges, if documents were faxed.**	
Sent To:	**Date:**	**Cost ($)**	**1st Minute**	**Each additional minute...**

CHAPTER FOUR

Fax Basics

Rᴇᴛᴀɪʟᴇʀꜱ, ꜰʀᴏᴍ ᴏꜰꜰɪᴄᴇ ꜱᴜᴘᴘʟʏ ꜱᴛᴏʀᴇꜱ ᴛᴏ ᴄᴀᴛᴀʟᴏɢᴜᴇ ꜱʜᴏᴡ rooms, have jumped on the fax bandwagon. Fueled by buyers' perception of fax as convenient and unobtrusive, fax is without question the hottest home/office machine. Because the fax machine is so easy to incorporate into one's work routine, those who use a fax can't imagine doing without one. However, the fax bandwagon is not without a few sour notes. The sour notes come primarily from marketing hype that leads buyers to the wrong purchase decisions.

LOW PRICE—THE COSTLY MISTAKE

Most office supply and equipment advertisements and discount showroom catalogues feature fax machines offered at considerable discounts. "Low-end," basic fax units at very modest prices are used to entice buyers into the store. Certainly price is important, but the most important consideration should be purchasing a machine that will best meet present and future fax needs. Sales personnel interviewed for this book remarked that many fax buyers respond solely to marketing tactics such as window displays featuring "Fax machines as low as . . ." Uninformed, impulse shoppers are the salesperson's dream customer . . . sell them low and soon they'll be back for a better unit—and that's what happens.

This chapter will help the reader understand the basic features found on today's Group III fax machines. An understanding of these features will not only help the buyer make a wise purchase decision, but also will help him/her obtain the maximum benefits from the machine once it's put into service. Chapter Five explores advanced fax features.

FAX BASICS

All fax machines are not alike, and not all machines will serve the needs of every fax user. From basic to full-featured units, fax manufacturers provide the user with a wide range of options and features. An understanding of basic fax features will help the buyer select from the wide range of fax units now offered for sale. A knowledge of basic fax enables the buyer to view more advanced features as either manufacturer hype or important in meeting his/her fax needs, both now and in the near future. Remember—fax is getting bigger and better.

☎ *Send legal forms in seconds.*

The Compatibility Factor

All Group III fax machines can communicate among one another; they're compatible. Most of these machines can also communicate to older fax units, especially Group II machines. The standards for Group III units were established by the CCITT or the Consultative Committee on International Telephone and Telegraph. This committee established the minimum speeds at which these machines communicate. (See Chapter Two for additional details about groups.)

Although many Group III machines have the ability to communicate with Group II and some Group I machines, not all Group II and I machines are able to communicate with Group III units. When communicating with Group II machines, for example, keep in mind that the print quality is not as good as that from Group III units. And not all Group III machines communicate at the fastest rate (9,600 bps). Communicating with slower machines means longer transmission times. Also, when communicating between Group III machines, certain features such as image reduction are dependent on the sending unit. The receiving unit will print out what it receives.

Transmission Speed

Communication time between fax machines is dependent not only upon machine compatibility and transmission line quality but also the amount of text, graphics, and/or photos being transmitted. *Fine* mode and *halftone* mode (used for photographs) take longer to transmit—they simply send more information.

To avoid the fax speed trap, remember that many of the advertisements touting incredibly short transmission times (such as nine seconds) are determined using pages with a minimum of text. In addition, fax transmission speed ratings provided by manufacturers generally do not take into account the time it takes for two fax machines to establish a communications link or "handshake." It typically takes about 15 seconds to establish the communications link. Therefore, transmission speed ratings should be used only as a guide. If you plan on typically sending and receiving pages dense with text and graphics, transmission times are going to be considerably longer than the fastest/shortest transmission times listed by most manufacturers.

IMAGE QUALITY

The amount of detail found in a fax transmission is dependent upon the resolution factors of the fax machine, in other words, the number of dots per inch. Standards for Group III units require both a regular and fine transmission mode.

Regular *normal mode* transmission provides 203 horizontal lines per inch and 98 vertical lines per inch, expressed as 203 X 98 DPL (dots per line). Group III fax has a normal resolution of 98 dots per inch of horizontal line. The greater the number of dots, the sharper the image.

Fine mode assures sharp transmission of documents with small print or greater detail such as shaded drawings and photos. Fine mode provides transmission with the same 203 horizontal lines per inch but offers dots at half the normal size, or 196 dots per horizontal inch. Fine mode takes longer to transmit.

Transmission quality is influenced by other factors such as line noise and the overall quality of the connections. Weather conditions can also influence the quality of transmission. To prevent damage to fax equipment, it is a good idea to use a surge protector on both the power supply and telephone connection. (See Chapter Ten for maintenance and preventive measures for fax machines.)

Thermal vs Plain Paper

Most fax machines use special heat-sensitive or thermal paper. Thermal paper is a specially coated paper that is very sensitive to heat. As the paper contacts a heat bar within the fax, the paper turns dark according to the intensity of heat and prints a dot pattern determined by the transmission received.

Some Group III machines use plain paper for printing. The process is very similar to that of a copier machine. Thermal printing is by far the most popular printing method. And thermal printing doesn't require toner or toner cartridges, ribbons or print heads. Plain paper printers are expensive, especially laser printers.

Thermal paper comes in rolls and must be cut into respective pages as it comes out of the fax machine. Some machines offer an optional paper cutter—a wise investment for those receiving many or multipage fax transmissions.

Document Size Limitations

Although most machines have a minimum document size of 5 inches by 5.8 inches, maximum original size specifications could be limiting for some users. Most machines accept documents up to 8.5 inches wide, and these are fine for most users. Should you require a machine that accepts originals wider than 8.5 inches, make sure it has *automatic reduction*. Auto reduction ensures that a receiving fax that cannot print on paper larger than 8.5 inches can receive the document and print it.

The maximum width of document content, or image area that the machine can read and transmit is the *effective scanning width*. Most machines can scan areas up to 8.3 inches wide. Originals 8.5 inches wide with an edge-to-edge image will suffer image loss on the copy. Some machines offer scanning widths of more than 10 inches.

Closely tied to effective scanning width is *effective printing width*. Although most fax machines utilize paper that is 8.5 inches wide, they print an image area up to 8.3 inches wide. Many machines automatically reduce images exceeding the 8.3 inches so that no image area is lost or clipped.

Paper Capacity

Roll paper is standard in current fax machines. Since thermal paper is thinner than most bond papers, it tends to curl easily. Thermal paper makes it possible to receive documents longer than 11 inches with no difficulty. However, a busy fax user will benefit greatly from an automatic paper cutter.

Most fax machines accommodate rolls of paper approximately 100 feet in length. Longer roll sizes are available, but the fax machine must be able to accommodate the larger size. Some fax machines will warn the user when paper supply is getting low. Roll replacement is simple and requires no messy liquids or toners.

BASIC OPERATION

Besides image quality and transmission rates, fax machines share common operating procedures—all fax machines can receive and transmit documents. Depending upon model and features, they differ in the sophistication of these operations.

Unattended Operation

A basic feature common to all fax machines is the ability to receive transmissions unattended. A sending fax machine calls the receiving machine and the document is printed as it is received.

Manufacturers have extended unattended operation to include an array of fax machine features based upon such operation.

To operate unattended, the fax machine must be able to answer the telephone. Therefore, unless the fax is on a phone line by itself (dedicated phone line) it must have a voice/data switch to change from telephone operation to fax mode. Some machines identify this as manual/automatic mode.

Built-in Handset

Some fax machines do not include a telephone handset, instead the user must provide a telephone that is easily connected to a telephone jack on the fax unit. A built-in handset makes a fax machine more versatile—the user can use the telephone to talk with another party or to dial another fax machine. A built-in handset is a valuable feature on even the most basic unit.

Copier Function

A fax machine can double as an inexpensive office copier. Instead of transmitting to another fax machine, the fax machine prints a copy of what its scanner reads. Although thermal copies are not as good nor as durable as plain paper office copiers, fax machines bring the convenience of a personal copier without the price. As with fax transmissions, most fax machines copy only single sheets of paper. Bound or multipage documents cannot be scanned or copied by the fax unit.

Desktop or Portable?

Whether it's a full-featured or a basic model, the desktop fax is affordable, easy to use and built to last. No larger than a portable typewriter, the desktop fax unit can be accommodated in even the most space-conscious office or home.

The popularity of the cellular car phone and the busy executive who travels from city to city has led to the emergence of the portable fax machine. Weighing in at about 10 pounds, the portable fax enables the busy executive to fax orders from a car with a cellular car phone or from a hotel room telephone via an acoustic coupler. (An acoustic coupler is a type of cradle that the handset of the telephone is placed in. The fax machine then communicates via the handset and cradle rather than plugging directly into a phone jack. Most hotel room telephones do not use modular telephone jacks. Instead, they are wired directly to the telephone line jacks.)

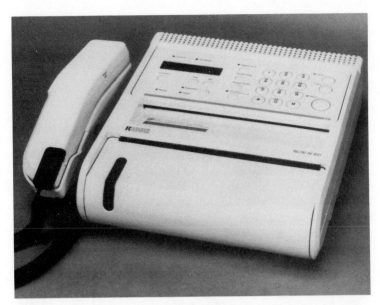

☎ *Ricoh's RF 800 personal facsimile/phone unit serves as both a fax and a voice phone. An optional carrying case makes it easy to take along on business trips. (Courtesy of Ricoh Corporation)*

The question for the potential fax buyer remains one of use. If the fax machine will be used primarily in one location, then the desktop fax is the wise decision. If the user needs to communicate while on the road throughout the business day and/or from temporary locations such as hotel rooms or a remote job site, then the portable fax is the answer. User needs determine choice.

Options Plus

Convenience, functionality, and affordable pricing have pushed the fax machine into the office mainstream. No longer a frilly option, fax machine manufacturers have responded to the increased demands for more flexible, feature-laden units. Chapter Five examines advanced fax features.

CHAPTER FIVE

Advanced Fax Features

A FULL-FEATURED FAX MACHINE CAN SAVE MONEY FOR THE FAX user by reducing transmission times, taking advantage of re-duced telephone rates at off-peak hours, and reducing or eliminat-ing fax operator time. Each enhanced feature has been carefully thought out and well planned to meet the ever increasing communi-cation needs and demands of today's busy executive, office worker, salesperson, and home-based businesses, as well as other con-sumers.

Long recognized for their ability to send documents over phone lines in a matter of seconds, it's just during the past few years that fax machines have been refined. These refinements have produced a lot of timesaving, expense-reducing features. But they have complicated the fax selection process.

The fax buyer is caught between brand names and the myriad of models offered by each manufacturer. Common questions arise such as:

❖ Which features will make business more efficient?
❖ Which features are just hype—bells and whistles?

Deciding upon the fax machine features you need most will be a lot less complicated if you keep in mind what various features enable you and the machine to do. The buyer must ask him/herself how he/she would benefit from the various features.

An enhanced feature can be placed into one or more of approximately five different groupings. Each group has a particular influence on the joy of fax. The fax feature groupings are:

❖ Features that reduce the impact of fax on telephone charges
❖ Features that reduce or eliminate fax machine operator time
❖ Features that ensure fax accuracy (receipt of transmission, etc.)
❖ Features that help improve copy quality
❖ Unique features that add flexibility and improve fax performance, especially for applications such as drafting, accounting, and design.

Some features fall into more than one group such as both time and speed. Other features fall primarily into one category. Certain features such as better copy quality can be both a benefit and somewhat of a hindrance—improved quality might result in increased transmission time. In such instances, there is a trade-off—speed for quality or accuracy.

FEATURES THAT HELP
LOWER CONNECT CHARGES

Since money is important to almost everyone, especially your long distance telephone carrier, features that can help reduce the cost of a fax transmission are usually critical to the dollar-conscious fax user. Manufacturers have been very responsive to the need for cost-effective fax transmissions.

Delayed Faxing/Dialing

Delayed dialing/sending is a feature formerly available only on high-end business fax machines. This money-saving feature enables the fax user to load documents into the fax machine's document feeder or memory and instruct the machine to send the items when phone rates are lower. Besides taking advantage of off-peak, discounted long-distance phone rates, delayed dialing enables a fax machine to use a nondedicated phone line (one used for regular telephone calls during business hours) after normal business hours.

Delayed Polling

Delayed polling enables a fax machine to call another fax at a predetermined time, ask if it has a document to send, and "pull" the document from the remote fax. Delayed polling makes it easy to take advantage of off-peak, discounted phone rates, and it doesn't require anyone be present at either machine. When polling, each machine must have a matching ID code that authorizes the exchange of documents. If the ID codes don't match, no exchange takes place.

Delayed Broadcasting

Delayed broadcasting enables a fax machine to take advantage of off-peak long-distance phone rates when the user needs to send the same documents to multiple locations. The documents are loaded into the memory of the fax machine, and the fax automatically begins calling other fax machines and sending the documents at a predetermined time.

Delayed broadcasting enables the machine to be used for receiving and sending other transmissions while waiting to broadcast. Some manufacturers allow the user to increase the capacity of the machine's memory by installing snap-in memory cartridges.

Transfer Request and Transfer Broadcast

Transfer request enables the fax user to send the same documents to several locations with just one phone call. Instead of calling each machine individually, the documents are sent to a host machine with *transfer broadcast* capability. The host machine will then send the document to other locations automatically. This feature can be particularly cost effective when the host unit is in the same dialing area.

Many of the fax services offered by companies such as MCI offer transfer request and/or transfer broadcast services without the sender having any specially equipped fax machine. CompuServe offers a similar fax service to computer users.

Turnaround Polling

Turnaround polling reduces the number of calls required when polling, delayed sending, or broadcasting to other fax machines. After sending documents, the fax machine determines if there are any documents waiting to be sent at the other end. If the other

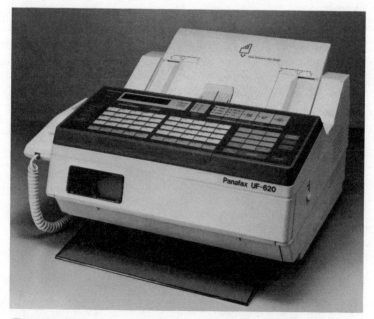

☎ *The Panafax UF-620 fax machine is a top-of-the-line unit that features 60-page memory and error correction mode. (Courtesy of Panafax Corporation)*

machine has a document for the sending unit, the machine automatically requests transmission of the document(s).

Voice Request

Voice request enables the sending party to notify the receiving party to pick up the handset either before or after a document is transmitted. Some machines identify voice request with a talk button. A fax machine must recognize the voice request signal in order to notify the other party to pick up the phone. A machine equipped with voice request capability will ring after or before fax transmission takes place.

FEATURES THAT REDUCE FAX OPERATOR TIME

The following features take fax users out of the fax line and help to expedite the fax process. With more and more people faxing documents, the line at the fax has joined the line at the copier. Whether a single fax user or one of many sharing a common fax, several features take the wait out of faxing.

Automatic Send and Receive

Most desktop fax machines have *automatic send and receive* capabilities. To automatically send documents, fax machines need a document feeder plus the delayed dialing and automatic disconnect features. All fax machines can automatically answer the phone, receive incoming fax documents, and disconnect at the end of the transmission.

Virtually all fax units enable the user to switch between automatic fax mode and telephone mode. Fax mode is most convenient for receiving transmissions unattended. Otherwise, you must manually push the send or start button to transmit or receive a document. In manual mode when dialing via a separate telephone or the built-in handset, you must place the phone in its cradle after the receiving fax machine has broadcast its connection signals. Automatic send and receive makes fax communication a lot easier.

One-Touch Dialing or Auto Dialer

One-touch or *auto dialing* permits the user to store frequently used phone numbers in the machine's memory, and transmit to those locations by loading the document and pressing a button.

One-touch dialing eliminates the need to look up frequently called numbers and eliminates misdialed numbers. Many units store up to 100 phone numbers.

Most auto dial functions let the user program instructions such as pausing when calling through switchboards or when using long-distance services that require a pause. Auto dial enhances the fax communication process through convenience and fast dialing speed.

Coded Dialing

Coded dialing is a natural complement to one-touch dialing. Coded dialing permits the user to store phone numbers in the machine's memory and access them by pressing a two-digit number.

Some fax machines, such as Canon, let the user assign a two-digit code for either a fax or telephone number. The fax machine's coded dialing differentiates between a fax call and regular telephone call by checking to see if a document has been inserted into the machine prior to dialing. (Note: When using speed dialing or coded dialing, make sure you know how to enter pauses when programming numbers for overseas calls or calls that require a pause prior to dialing.)

Group Dial Capability

Group dial enables a fax machine to store groups of phone numbers for polling, broadcast or transfer request applications. Many units permit the storage of instructions for frequent operations—such as polling a group of fax machines at a set time.

Broadcasting

Broadcasting is particularly handy for those who must send the same document(s) to a number of fax units. The original is loaded into the sending fax's memory. Because the document is in memory, the user doesn't need to stay near the machine and feed the same document over and over. The machine automatically sends the document(s) to each location specified, thus freeing the fax machine user for other tasks. (See "Delayed Broadcasting.")

Automatic Redial

Automatic redial or *resend* eliminates manually resending documents if a machine with this feature reaches a busy signal or encounters telephone line problems. These machines can redial the busy number(s) up to a user-selectable number of times. Usually an error report is printed after a certain number of redial attempts.

Ricoh fax machines, for example, automatically resend all or part of a document from memory when it detects an error signal from the receiving end. Such a feature helps ensure receipt of all pages.

On some fax machines, this feature operates in conjunction with broadcast and group dial operations. When a busy signal or line difficulty is encountered, the machine will proceed down the dial list and go back and redial numbers to which it was unable to transmit.

Last-Number Redial

Last-number redial lets the user rering the last number dialed by pushing a button. This feature works for both fax calls and regular telephone calls.

Alternate Number Dial

Alternate number dial is useful when important documents must get through to the other party. The fax machine automatically dials a "backup" number when the first number is busy.

Memory Storage and Backup

Memory-equipped fax machines can electronically "store and forward" pages of text for later transmission. If a memory-equipped fax runs out of paper, it can automatically store incoming documents and print them out after the unit is reloaded with paper. Memory capability also enables a fax machine to broadcast the same documents to several machines. (See "Broadcasting.")

Polling

Polling enables one fax machine to call another, ask if it has a document to send, and "pull" the document from the other fax. (See "Delayed Polling.")

Automatic Document Feeder

Automatic document feeding is found on all but the most basic fax machines. This feature enables the machine to send multipage documents unattended by working in conjunction with automatic dialing to send documents automatically. It eliminates time-consuming hand feeding of documents.

Machines vary in the reliability of automatic document feeding, as well as the number of pages that can be stacked in the feeder. It is strongly suggested that the user check out the operation of this feature prior to purchase.

Automatic Paper Cutter

An *automatic paper cutter* enables the machine to automatically cut each incoming transmission to the length of the original. Also, an automatic paper cutter facilitates the reception of numerous consecutive transmissions and multipage documents. The user doesn't spend time tearing off individual copies or cutting apart pages from one long, continuous sheet of paper. This feature helps keep papers neat and orderly.

Dual Access

Dual access eliminates waiting for a reception or transmission to end in order to use the fax machine. This feature lets you immediately store one or more sets of documents with instructions in memory . . . while the unit is also receiving. If the unit is sending, the user can place documents in the feeder and enter instructions. The fax machine will automatically send the documents when the previous transmission or reception ends. (See "Reserve Next Operation.")

Reserve Next Operation

Reserve next operation is a limited form of dual access where the fax machine can be used while it is receiving a document without the need for memory. Documents are placed in the auto feeder and directions entered. When the machine is through receiving, it automatically starts the reserved operation.

Monitor Speaker

A *monitor speaker* frees the operator's hands and ensures that the transmission is proceeding without difficulty. The speaker lets the user hear when a busy signal is reached or if someone answers the call instead of a fax machine.

FEATURES THAT ENSURE FAX ACCURACY AND CONTROL ACCESS

Line noise, busy signals, and misfeed of originals are just a few of the things that can affect the accuracy of a fax transmission. Besides accuracy, it is often important that sensitive information be restricted.

Manufacturers have built-in many features that help ensure documents arrive and that those documents of confidential nature are seen only by those with authorization. This section examines such features.

Management Reports

Fax machines keep track of transmissions, both sending and receiving, through a built-in transmission log. Units print management reports on demand or after a specified number of transmissions. Reports list the calls made, time, destination, origination, connect time, and other user information.

Transmit Terminal Identification

Transmit terminal identification lets the receiving party know who sent the transmission, when it was sent, and the page number. The sending fax machine automatically sends this information along with each page. The receiving fax prints the information at the head of each page of the faxed document.

Remote Terminal Identification

Remote terminal identification ensures that the fax is being sent to the correct location before the documents are sent. The receiving fax user can also see who is sending a document. Remote terminal identification causes the fax number or terminal ID label of the other fax unit to be displayed on the readout display screen.

Transaction Confirmation Report

Management reports usually indicate both transmission and receptions, indicating date, time, ID of other unit, length of transaction and result (transmission OK or error). (See "Management Reports.")

Confidential Transmission/Confidential Reception/ Personal Password

Confidential transmission and *confidential reception* help maintain confidentiality of sensitive documents. The fax machine directs documents into the memory of a unit rather than printing them out. The documents are printed only when the correct password is entered.

Some machines offer the use of a *personal password* for a higher level of confidentiality. The sending party enters a personal password with the transmission instructions. An individual at the receiving end must enter the sender's password to print those documents.

Error Report

If a fax machine with *error report* capabilities encounters difficulty either receiving or sending a transmission, the machine will identify any problems by printing an error report. When transmitting, affected pages are identified and the problem identified, then the affected pages are re-sent.

Restricted Access

Restricted access is a particularly valuable feature for use in offices. This features helps avoid unauthorized or careless use by requiring an ID code or magnetic card. The fax machine will not accept any instructions until a valid code or card is entered.

Secure Polling

Secure polling restricts outside polling of a fax unit to only those machines with a matching access code. This feature prevents unauthorized "pickup."

Code override maintains security when polling codes are different without reprogramming the fax. This feature enables the user to override the present code by entering another machine's code during setup.

Error Correction Mode

Units with *error correction mode* (ECM) automatically resend a document if line noise has garbled the transmission. ECM helps ensure copy quality/accuracy.

Remote Diagnostics

Some fax machine manufacturers offer *remote diagnostics* to help keep machine downtime to a minimum. A service department can test and correct most common problems over the phone, eliminating the cost and wait for field service.

FEATURES THAT IMPROVE COPY QUALITY

Since the purpose of faxing is to share information with another location, the image quality of the copy received determines if the message is understood. Manufacturers offer several fax machine features to help ensure that copy remains clear and legible.

Contrast Document Enhancement Control

Contrast document enhancement control helps to maintain the legibility of documents with dark-colored backgrounds and permits users to increase the sharpness of poor quality originals. Manual contrast control is preferable to automatic because it enables the user to adjust the contrast much like a copy machine.

Detail Mode

Detail mode offers improved reproduction quality with only a slight reduction in transmission speed. The user usually switches the detail mode between *normal* and *fine*. Fine or high resolution mode is useful to enhance fine print, complex graphics, or photographs.

Halftone Mode

Although *halftone mode* slows transmission, it significantly improves the reproduction of photographs or shaded sketches. Most fax machines break down a photo into 8 or 16 different shades of gray. A few machines provide an incredible 64 shades of gray. (See "Adjustable Gray Scale.")

Adjustable Gray Scale

Most fax machines offer the user *gray scale adjustment* for better reproduction of photographs and drawings. This adjustment should be used cautiously because it increases transmission time, and if improperly adjusted, it can result in good-quality graphics but borderline text quality.

☎ *A host of sophisticated functions including sequential broadcast, delayed transmission, a programmable outgoing message, and halftone transmission capabilities equip the FaxPhone 25 to handle even the most demanding communications needs. (Courtesy of Canon U.S.A., Inc.)*

Copy Mode

Copy mode helps the user ensure the clarity of a document before it is faxed. Review a copy printed by the machine and make adjustments to the settings if necessary. Copy mode also lets the fax machine double as a "backup" copier.

Smoothing Image Correction

Smoothing image correction helps reduce the jaggedness in transmission copy. This correction "smooths out" the copy image for a more accurate representation of the original, and copy appears as though it was sent in fine mode.

Automatic Step Down

Virtually all Group III fax machines have *automatic step down*. The fax detects when the telephone line cannot support a higher transmission speed. The fax's modem automatically slows down the speed of the transmission to a speed the line can accommodate. Slower speeds are usually necessary when communicating over noisy telephone lines and/or when poor quality telephone connections exist.

SPECIAL-PURPOSE FAX FEATURES

Although most fax users find the features found on the majority of fax machines more than adequate, those users with unique fax needs have not been forgotten. Architects, accountants, and others who use paper that is wider than 8.5 inches as well as those wishing to connect a fax machine to their computer should find this section most informative.

Wide Scanning Width

A *wide scanning width* enables the user to send wide documents without reducing them first on a copier or cutting them into sections. Some machines can accommodate originals as wide as 10.1 inches and others can transmit computer printouts and ledgers. The copy is automatically reduced to fit the paper in the receiving unit.

If you normally send documents on wide paper, check the effective scanning width as well as maximum original size and effective print width of the fax machine prior to purchase.

Effective Printing Width

Some fax machines accommodate wide paper for printing documents that cannot be reduced or the user does not want reduced. Such machines are considerably more expensive. (See "Wide Scanning Width.")

Recorded Voice Announcement

A *recorded voice announcement* greets callers with a recorded message that they have dialed a fax machine instead of greeting them with the sound of the fax machine trying to "handshake" with another fax. The voice announcement can also direct callers to another number for regular phone calls.

Automatic Answering Machine

The *automatic answering machine* feature is relatively new on fax machines. This makes the desktop fax unit a combination answering machine, fax machine, and copier. In automatic mode, the fax machine greets callers with a recorded message, and if it does not detect a voice within several seconds after playing the recorded message, the machine switches to fax mode and can receive a fax transmission.

Portable Fax

The *portable fax* is a full-featured fax that can travel with the user. These units can be used in a hotel room via a built-in acoustic coupler (most hotel room telephones do not use modular telephone jacks). Many portable fax machines can be used with a cellular car phone with the proper adapter(s).

RS232-C Interface

An RS232-C interface permits the fax machine to be used as a printer for a personal computer or as an image scanner for inputting documents into a personal computer. The user must have the appropriate connecting cable and software.

FAX COMPARISON CHART

The fax comparison chart identifies the most common features found on desktop fax machines. Space is provided at the top of the chart to record the manufacturers, models, and prices of various fax units. Note those features most important to you. As you shop and

Fax Machine Comparison Chart				
Manufacturer:				
Model:				
Price:				
Features:				
Dimensions				
Autodialer Capacity				
Auto Redial				
Coded Dialing				
Delayed Send				
Memory (in pages)				
Error Correction				

Auto Fallback				
Transmission Confirmation				
Auto Document Feed				
Halftone				
Fine Mode				
Reduction				
Auto Reduction				
Polling				
Poll Later				
Sequential Polling				
Voice Identification				
Answering Machine				
Confidential Transmission				
Confidential Reception				
On Hook Dial				
Built-in Handset				
Monitor Speaker				
Group II and III				
Group I compatible				
Quick Dial				
Group Dial				
Group List				
Maximum # pages Auto Feed				
Substitute Reception				
Smoothing Function				
Sequential Broadcast				
Memory List				
Display Type				
Indicator Lamps				
On/Off Switch				
Replace Roll Indicator				
Top Loading				
Front Loading				
Built-in Keypad				
Handset Keypad				
Contrast Adjustment				
Adjustable Paper Guide				
Password				
Gray Scale				
Transmission Time Minimum				
Resolution — Standard				
Resolution — Fine				
Scanning/Max. Width				
Scanning/Min. Width				
Printing/Max. Width				
Output Document Size				
Paper Roll				
Scanner Type				
Warranty				
On-line Diagnostics				

compare different machines, check off and compare the features on those units considered for purchase.

Confusion Factor

As the fax arena becomes increasingly more competitive, manufacturers will become increasingly more aggressive as they try to grab the potential fax buyer. As a consumer, the fax buyer needs to be informed. He/she needs to understand the various fax features and what they can do for him/her. By understanding how the various features can benefit the user, the buyer can better evaluate the performance of a particular brand or model of fax machine. But even more important than understanding product literature and machine specifications, the buyer must understand his/her own fax needs.

Understanding one's fax needs requires more than selecting a machine that can fulfill a basic request such as, "I need to send documents quickly." Understanding your fax needs means knowing the answers to questions such as:

❖ How often do you need documents delivered as soon as possible?

❖ Have you had others request or ask if you can fax something to them?

❖ Do you regularly work around tight or inflexible deadlines?

❖ Do your information sources such as libraries offer fax service?

❖ Do you have a dedicated telephone line just for a fax machine?

❖ Can you fax documents to others after hours when long-distance phone rates are less?

Although some of these questions might sound as though you're trying to decide if you really need a fax machine, the answers to many of these questions will actually help you and a salesperson determine the level of fax capabilities you require. Few people involved in any type of timely business can escape having a fax machine. Owning or having access to a fax is becoming the status quo.

The fax features required to meet the user's needs can range from a bare-bones fax model to a feature-laden unit that can send the same documents unattended to 25 remote fax machines, over a regular (nondedicated) phone line, after regular business hours. By taking a close look at present communications (telephone charges, courier service, overnight delivery of documents, and E-mail), the buyer and a "knowledgeable" salesperson should be able to pinpoint those fax units that best meet fax needs both now and in the future.

Time spent evaluating user expectations, user needs, and how various model fax machines address those needs is time well spent. In some instances, using a fax machine on a regular basis has not only improved service; using a fax has increased profits by lowering the cost of doing business.

Evaluation Pointer

A good test of the capabilities of a fax machine is a real-life demonstration. This does not mean having the salesperson use the copier function of the machine to demonstrate the image quality of a copy. An accurate and realistic demonstration should include an actual fax transmission using all features such as send later, broadcast simulation, etc. The buyer should provide samples of actual documents that he/she will fax using the machine. A good indicator of text quality is a page from a telephone directory. Photographs from magazines and/or product photos can provide an indication of gray-scale capabilities as well as the time it takes to transmit more complex documents.

(Note: Most fax specification charts should be used as general guides only. Often the transmission times are derived from performance tests that use test documents containing a minimal amount of text and/or graphics. Typically, the average fax transmission contains far more information than test documents used by manufacturers. The buyer should provide his/her own samples to more realistically evaluate transmission times for various fax machines.)

The Fax Advantage

Acquiring the fax machine that can best meet individual or business needs is the first step in realizing the fax advantage. Implementing the use of that machine and understanding and exploiting its capabilities are necessary to derive the most benefits from the unit. Once the machine is acquired, the buyer must consider how to best benefit from the purchase/lease. Chapter Six explores making the fax connections.

CHAPTER SIX

Setting Up a Fax Machine

Of PRIMARY IMPORTANCE TO THE OWNER OF ANY NEW PRODUCT
is how to use it. If the fax buyer has given careful consideration to his/her fax needs and selected a machine that is capable of
meeting those needs, the next task is to understand how to get the
machine to do all that it was designed to do. But before the unit is
connected to the power and phone lines, the user needs to give
thought to the following:

❖ Where do you want to locate the unit?
❖ Is adequate electrical power available (outlets, too many devices
on the same circuit)?
❖ Is a telephone jack accessible?
❖ Do you need to have a dedicated telephone line installed for the
fax machine?
❖ In a small or medium-sized office, who is going to be responsible for the machine?
❖ Who will ensure that office staff know how to operate, trou-
bleshoot and understand error messages and load paper into the
machine when necessary?

LOCATION, LOCATION . . .

The location of the fax machine should be of prime importance
to users and management. Since the goal of having a fax machine is

to communicate more effectively, the convenience of having a fax machine readily accessible can and will influence how effectively the unit is used.

If users must maneuver around a busy secretary's or receptionist's work area, negative feelings will eventually develop toward using the machine. The machine should not be considered an intruder, nor should the fax user be an intruder into another's work area. A mutually satisfying location for the fax machine can foster optimal use of the machine.

A fax machine should not be placed in an area where it will be exposed to dust, vibration, high humidity, direct sunlight, or heat from sources such as heater ducts or from sitting on top of heat-generating equipment. Likewise, do not place the unit on a shelf or inside a cabinet that might prevent adequate ventilation around the unit. Besides the sensitive electronic components inside the fax machine, heat will damage documents; the excessive heat causes thermal paper to turn black.

☎ *Demco offers a line of sturdy, highly functional, and attractive fax machine stands. (Courtesy of Demco, Inc.)*

POWER REQUIREMENTS

Fax machines require no more power than an ordinary electric typewriter or personal computer: standard 120V ac household current. Unfortunately, a common misconception about most office equipment is that the user merely has to plug the unit into an ordinary electric outlet and turn on the machine. Power requirements are a very serious issue in today's office.

The electronic components in most of today's office equipment require very little electrical power, but these components are incredibly sensitive to variations in voltage and power line surges. Therefore, the fax machine should not share a power outlet with other appliances that cause electrical "noise." Air conditioners, electric typewriters, copiers, and machines of this sort generate noise that often interferes with sending and receiving fax documents.

Besides an electric outlet with ample power, electronic office equipment should have surge and voltage protectors. These protectors clip or cut off surges and spikes in power lines that can damage equipment within fractions of a second. Even a window air conditioner can wreak havoc with the circuits of a fax machine. Curtis is one manufacturer that offers effective and safe surge protection units that merely plug into the wall outlet.

☎ *The SAFE-Fax is a single outlet phone line and ac line surge protector for economical protection against dangerous high-voltage surges in phone and ac power lines. (Courtesy of Curtis Manufacturing Company, Inc.)*

In addition to an adequate power supply, fax machines require that the power remain on at all times. Even if the fax machine is used in manual mode only, the memory of the fax machine requires power in order to retain program information, i.e., phone and fax numbers, transmission information, date, and time.

Make sure the fax is connected to an electrical outlet that remains on at all times. Many users have inadvertently killed the power to their machine when leaving for the day by flipping off the lights. When power to the machine is turned off, the machine cannot operate unattended and will not retain information in its memory.

CONNECTING TO THE TELEPHONE LINE

There are two basic installation options when connecting a fax to telephone lines. The fax machine can have its own dedicated telephone line, which many telephone companies offer at a reduced rate. Or, the fax machine can share a line with household or business phones.

Whether the user decides to connect the fax to a dedicated or shared phone line, the machine must be within reach of a telephone

☎ *Radio Shack offers a complete line of telephone connectors, wires, and other accessories that make installing an extra telephone jack easy. (Courtesy of Radio Shack)*

jack. If you require a dedicated telephone line, the telephone company will install the line and jack. However, if you decide to use an existing phone line, you can readily find the proper tools and connectors at most electronic stores.

An important point concerning the use of a dedicated versus a shared phone line is availability. Using a telephone on a shared line will tie up the line on the fax machine (no fax transmission can occur when the line is being used for voice phone calls) and vice versa. Also, if a telephone on a shared line is picked up while fax transmission is taking place, the fax transmission will halt and an error report will be printed. A dedicated phone line will alleviate such problems.

Connect a Phone and Fax to a Single Line

Electronic Speech Systems, Inc. offers an affordable alternative to the dedicated phone line by making it possible for a telephone and fax machine to share the same single telephone line. Fax/Phone Switch II is a state-of-the-art accessory that eliminates the need for a dedicated phone line and the wait for installation.

The Fax/Phone Switch II automatically and quietly distinguishes between voice and data signals, switching calls to the tele-

☎ *The Fax/Phone Switch II automatically distinguishes between voice and fax calls, eliminating the need for a dedicated phone line. (Courtesy of Electronic Speech Systems, Inc.)*

phone, fax or a computer modem (fax modem). There are no buttons to push and no calls to transfer. On incoming calls, all the user need do is answer the telephone or read his/her fax. On outgoing calls, the fax, modem, and phone all work as they would on dedicated phone lines.

The unit saves on costly telephone installation fees and monthly charges. It provides data integrity and manages the phone line, letting the user know when the line is busy during a data transmission. Best of all, the unit is easy to install and use.

How Does the Fax/Phone Switch II Work?

On outgoing calls, the switch senses whether the phone or fax (or modem) goes off the hook and connects the unit making the outgoing call to the phone line. On incoming calls, the switch intercepts the call and says to the caller, "Hello. To reach our fax, please remain silent. To reach our phone, say 'telephone' at the tone." The incoming signals are then analyzed and determined to be silence or a fax/modem tone or speech.

If the switch detects silence or a fax/modem tone, it rings the local fax or modem. If it senses speech, it rings the local phone. When the ring is answered, the switch connects the incoming line to the appropriate device. Convenient, cost effective, and reliable, this device can even work with an answering machine.

Be sure that the telephone line to which a fax machine is connected does not have the "call waiting" feature. Call waiting momentarily disturbs fax transmissions and will result in either disconnect of the fax units or data errors on the printed output.

FAX RESPONSIBILITY

Fax junk mail has received a lot of bad press. But for those people who enjoy receiving advertisements in the mail, fax provides a new twist to an old idea (direct mail). However, whatever is received via the fax machine means that the machine is unavailable for authorized fax calls. Such calls also use fax paper, which means the receiver is paying for junk mail. In a busy office, junk mail requires operator time just as authorized fax mail. Therefore, be cautious of having fax numbers listed in various publications unless you accept the fact that unsolicited mail might start arriving.

Fax Security

Even before the machine is delivered, it should be determined who is going to be responsible for both using and tending to the machine. Accessibility is important for encouraging employees to use the device, but confidentiality is another important factor. Unless a fax machine is equipped with a security code or confidential transmission feature, fax documents have no protection from unauthorized reading. Therefore, an office might need to establish standard procedures for the receipt and delivery of documents. Some businesses use a specific color envelope to notify recipients that a fax document is enclosed. Others have a specific area or location where fax documents are placed as they are received.

Security, confidentiality, and accessibility are concerns for any business that has fax machines available for use. Many businesses spend a sizeable amount on nonbusiness fax transmissions because employees fax everything from lunch orders to requests for songs to radio stations. The small office might have more control over such factors than the large office; but fax responsibility should be a prime concern for all fax users whether sender or receiver.

Fax Master

It seems as though everyone wants to get in on the fax routine, especially when the machine is first put into operation. Every user should know more about the machine than just how to place or receive a call. Certain features such as "send later" and "polling" can save businesses large amounts of money. But if employees do not know about such capabilities or how to use them, what good are the features?

Every office, large or small, should have a core of individuals who are well versed in the operation of the fax machine and who can instruct others in the proper operation of the device. Users need to know what to do when the machine prints out an error report, how to correct paper jams, how to load paper into the machine, and other operational procedures.

Every fax purchase should include instruction in how to operate the device. Many companies will connect and test the equipment upon delivery. The person(s) identified as primary operator(s) should each receive initial hands-on training in how to operate the unit. They in turn should train other users.

GETTING TO KNOW THE FAX

Once a satisfactory location has been identified and the proper power outlets and phone lines are available, the next step is to set up the fax and test it. The user must get to know and understand how to work the unit.

Many people make the mistake of unpacking the fax machine and throwing away the carton and shipping materials, often without testing the equipment. Before attempting to install the machine, the first thing to do is pull out the owner's manual and go over the packing list to ensure that all the items were shipped with the unit. Retain all shipping materials should the unit need to be shipped for service or returned for exchange.

It is very tempting to just plug the machine in, connect it to the phone line, and dial away. Unfortunately, many people never perform the most important task for getting the most out of their fax machine, they neglect to read the owner's manual.

Usually the first task will be to load the machine with its initial supply of paper, followed by setting the sender ID information. Before attempting to register any information, take time to thoroughly study the diagrams and/or photos depicting the various controls of the machine, especially if the machine has more advanced features such as coded dialing, group dial, etc.

Once the user has identified all the components, location of controls, and properly connected the machine, the unit is ready for its first test. Usually, the first test is to copy a document using the fax's copy feature. This tests both scanning and printing features. Before actually conducting the test, be sure you know how to load an original document and that the recording paper is correctly loaded.

Chapter Seven offers hints and tips to help the reader get the most out of his/her fax machine. A thorough understanding of how to use the machine will ensure optimum performance and maximum efficiency.

Fax User Hints and Tips

A FAX MACHINE PROVIDES AN EASY WAY TO COMMUNICATE quickly, and using one to send documents can save money by lowering the cost of communicating. In addition, today's fax machines with fast transmission rates, the ability to operate unattended and take advantage of reduced telephone rates at off-peak hours, and features that reduce or eliminate fax operator time make faxing one of the most cost-effective and efficient ways to get the message across.

Whether a fax is used by small or large business, an individual, or an organization of individuals, there are basic pointers that all fax users should consider even before using their fax machine for the first time. The following hints and tips apply whether fax communications take place from around the corner or across the country. (*Tip:* Those who want to fax to locations outside of the United States might find the section on overseas fax communication helpful.)

PREPARING DOCUMENTS
FOR FAXING OR COPYING

Certain requirements and precautions should be observed before sending or copying documents via a fax machine. This is to ensure that they are properly sent and that the original documents don't jam in the machine.

Document Rules

Do not attempt to feed the following types of documents into the fax or they might jam. In some instances, you must first make photocopies and then feed the copies into the fax machine.

❖ Wrinkled or creased paper
❖ Curled or rolled paper
❖ Torn paper
❖ Carbon paper or carbon-backed paper
❖ Coated paper
❖ Onion skin or very thin paper

Remove clips, staples, or other similar objects from documents before feeding them into the fax machine. Let ink or paste on documents dry completely before placing them in the machine. And, check the owner's manual and identify maximum and minimum document sizes. If your machine has an auto feed feature, make sure not to exceed the maximum number of sheets the machine can handle. Use a photocopier to reduce oversize documents or to print documents that are too small to feed into the fax.

TESTING A NEW FAX

A good test document for a fax machine is a copy of a page from a standard telephone directory. This will help ensure satisfactory contrast and detail settings. Other good test documents include magazine pages. (If test pages are too flimsy and misfeed into the fax, make a copy of the document.)

If test transmissions are successful, proceed with installation and programming of telephone and fax numbers, as well as speed dial, coded dial, and other instructions (depending on your machine).

If test situations prove unsatisfactory, review basic operating instructions, check the chapter in this book on fax troubleshooting, and if necessary, return the unit for exchange or service.

THE FAX COVER SHEET

The power and speed at which a fax transmits and receives has had a great impact on business and the need for instantaneous communications. Some of us can no longer offer an acceptable excuse for documents arriving beyond deadline, and many of us find the fax actually helps us beat the deadline. Whether friend or foe, a fax document is only good if received.

The increased activity in fax mail has led to real concerns in many offices. When does a fax require immediate attention? How does a busy office keep track of all these urgent, faxed documents? The very fact that a document was faxed seems to imply urgency and/or importance. But many businesses also find faxing more efficient and less costly than traditional mail.

Even though the receiving fax machine might confirm receipt of a document, receipt by the recipient can only be ensured through measures taken on the receiving party's end. There are a number of ways to help ensure that fax documents reach their destination. The most goof-proof method is simultaneous manual sending and receiving or talking directly to the receiving party prior to and after sending a document—verbal confirmation. However, verbal confirmation negates the advantage of unattended transmissions and might not be possible.

A fax cover sheet is of prime importance when sending any document(s). Whether sending to a busy office or to an individual, a fax transmittal cover sheet lets the receiver know who sent it, how many pages it's comprised of, when it was sent, special attention and/or instructions, and a number to call with questions or notification of transmission difficulty.

A well-designed cover sheet should:

❖ Include the name and address of the sender in large type. The type used for most letterheads is too small and stylized to transmit properly. When uncertain as to how a letterhead will transmit, use the fax machine's copy feature to test for reproduction quality. Make necessary adjustments to standard/detail settings and contrast adjustment. Keep the cover sheet simple in design. Complex cover sheets with fancy borders, illustrations, etc. increase transmission time.

❖ Identify the recipient. This is especially important in locations where many individuals receive fax transmissions. And when faxing to a fax service, be sure to include the phone number of the recipient so the fax service can notify him/her that a document is waiting for pickup.

❖ Provide a subject category, e.g., orders, credit application, etc. A subject category helps direct documents to the proper department or group of individuals.

❖ Indicate the number of pages being transmitted. The number should include the cover sheet. This helps with collation at the receiving end, and it also enables the receiver to determine if any pages are missing.

✤ Inform the recipient of whom to contact should difficulty occur
during transmission or should questions arise.
✤ Include both a fax number and telephone number if both are
available.
✤ If the transmission is part of a group dial, inform recipients of
others who were copied by noting "c." or "forward," etc.

Gerald V. Quinn
29 Carolina Avenue
Trenton, NJ 08618
(609) 771–6984

FACSIMILE TRANSMITTAL COVER SHEET

Date: _____ Time: _____

PLEASE DELIVER THE FOLLOWING PAGES TO:
Name: _____
Fax Number: _____
Firm: _____
City: _____

FROM:
Gerald V. Quinn
Writing Consultant
Subject:_____

I AM TRANSMITTING ___ PAGES (including the cover sheet).

If you do not receive all of the pages indicated above
or if you experience difficulty with transmission,
call me at 609/771–6984.

If you wish to send a return transmission,
my FAX number is: **555/123-4567**

☎ *Facsimile Transmittal Cover Sheet*

It might be helpful to note the name of the document or indicate that a particular page is 1 of 10, for example. This way, the person receiving the documents can place them in the proper order. Remember that fax transmissions come out of the machine stacked in reverse order. A busy fax location could mean sorting through 50 or more fax transmission pages.

If you have a personal computer, you can use a page layout or drawing program to create an interesting, stylized, and easy-to-read fax transmittal cover sheet. SmartForms for the Macintosh is one program that lends itself to such specific applications.

Fax Memo Notes

The 3M Company, famous for Post-Its (those handy memo sheets used for everything from grocery lists to phone messages), has created Post-It Fax, which are transmittal memo notes that attach to a corner of transmitted documents. These notes provide space for information that is usually included on transmittal cover

☎ *3M Company's Post-It Fax transmittal memo notes attach to a corner of transmittal documents. These 1.5-by-4-inch notes provide space for information usually included on transmittal cover sheets and are printed with black ink on white paper for enhanced facsimile reproduction. (Courtesy of 3M Company)*

sheets and are printed on white paper for enhanced facsimile reproduction.

PUTTING FAX REPORTS TO WORK

Many fax machines can provide the user with useful information concerning transmissions as they take place. Such a fax machine is able to keep track of most of the activities it performs and print out reports of the activities for the user's records. This is convenient for confirming the exact date and time of communication, the volume of documents that have been processed, and other important information.

Activity Reports

The user can keep a record of the documents sent by having the fax machine print out *activity reports*. Each report shows the date and time of the transaction, the name and telephone number of the receiving party, the number of pages of the document, and other information.

Some fax machines such as those from Canon enable the user to instruct the machine to print out activity reports as determined by the user. For example, the FaxPhone 25 can print out an activity report every time a document is sent. Even if an error occurs or the other party failed to answer when the machine tried to send a document, the fax will print out a report so the other party can be contacted and an attempt to transmit can be made again.

Activity Management Reports

Most fax machines can provide a record of the last 20 or so sending and receiving transactions by printing out an *activity management report*. This can help keep track of fax usage for both sending and receiving, and it can help in determining the need for additional fax units.

Tip: From time to time, check your activity management reports for any facsimile numbers that you dialed using regular dialing. If the same numbers appear repeatedly, you might want to register them for either one-touch or coded speed dialing.

Broadcast Reports

If your machine has broadcast capability, you can keep records of transactions involving more than one other fax unit by having your machine print out *broadcast reports*. These reports show the one-touch speed dialing number used to dial the other party and whether or not the fax was able to successfully complete the transaction.

Most machines with broadcast capabilities can be programmed to print out a report each time it finishes sending a document to multiple locations. This provides a convenient way to document the transmission and receipt of important documents.

User Switches

User switch settings vary from unit to unit. The switch settings enable the user to control certain operations of the fax machine. These switches are actually settings that control such automatic features as paper cutting frequency, the off-hook alarm for the phone, report printouts, and other operations.

COMMUNICATING OVERSEAS

The speed at which communication takes place via a fax machine makes communication between the United States and foreign

☎ *Canon's ultra-compact FaxPhone 20 features a two-line liquid crystal display with interactive prompts. The unit is ideal for daily use at major corporations or home-based business. (Courtesy of Canon U.S.A., Inc.)*

countries an ideal candidate for faxing. However, there are certain facts that should be considered prior to attempting to fax overseas.

❖ Since any Group III fax machine is required by international standards to be able to communicate with any other Group III fax machine, international communication between fax machines is possible.

❖ A fax call can be placed to any country you can dial directly from your phone.

❖ Since fax transmission is dependent upon a distortion-free or noise-free line, you might experience transmission difficulties on lines to countries where telephone transmission normally experiences breakup or distortion. Communication to such countries could result in machines transmitting at the slowest speed possible, or you might experience error messages such as "no carrier detect" meaning the connection has been lost. Poor-quality phone lines can also result in data "hits" or white spots (transmission errors) on the printed copy.

❖ You might need to make repeated attempts to complete the transmission of multipage documents.

❖ Long-distance phone rates vary depending on the foreign country you are calling. Discount rates vary according to the time you are calling. Your long-distance telephone carrier can provide rate schedules. Since long-distance phone rates vary according to the time you wish to call, delayed calling (send later), delayed broadcasting, and delayed polling are just a few of the features found on many fax machines that are not only convenient but also prove cost effective and can easily save more than the initial cost of a fax machine.

❖ When operator assistance is required to call another country, be sure to tell the overseas operator that you are placing a "data" call. If you do not inform the operator that you wish to make a "data" call, the operator will come on the line to verify the call and you will lose the carrier (other fax machine). When the operator is informed of a "data" call, the other fax machine will be able to establish proper sequence and phasing (handshake) with the calling machine, and transmission will proceed without interruption.

❖ You cannot purchase a fax machine in the United States and ship that machine to another country. Besides import/export regulations, most countries require local government certification before a fax machine can be connected to phone lines. "Type" approval is required for equipment to be connected to the local public telephone network. Different power and transmission standards in each country require equipment modification to ensure optimal operation.

❖ You cannot purchase a fax machine outside of the United States and expect it to operate in the United States. Power and transmission standards are different in other countries, and a non-U.S. standard fax machine might not operate properly and could result in damage to the equipment. Even though a fax machine bears the same brand name and might even be the same in appearance as a unit offered for sale in the United States, differences in manufacturing specifications for power and transmission standards could render the unit inoperable in the U.S. and pose a serious safety hazard.

In the United States, most of the overseas fax transmissions occur between the United States and Japan. This is due to the fact that so many Japanese companies have corporate offices based in the United States.

Communication between foreign countries can be greatly enhanced via the fax machine because the fax machine either eliminates or minimizes the language barrier, both written and spoken. A document can be written in Japanese, for example, and sent as is via a fax. Also, because the document arrives instantly, more time can be spent translating documents, if needed. The person receiving the fax transmission needn't be present, and unlike a voice call between individuals who speak different languages, an intepreter isn't needed (at least to receive the document).

As new users become more acquainted and comfortable operating a fax machine, they usually begin to wonder how they got along without it. The more fax is used, the more useful it becomes. Chapter Eight examines how to expand the usefulness of fax technology by combining the power of the personal computer with that of the fax machine.

CHAPTER EIGHT

The PC-Fax Connection

LITTLE MORE THAN TEN YEARS AGO, YOU ASKED THE OPERATOR for information—when you needed a telephone number. Today, *information* means far more than a telephone number, and it isn't something that's nice to have—it's expected. Modern technology places enormous amounts of information right at everyone's fingertips. Granted, you might need a personal computer, telephone, or a good friend at the library to find what you need or want to know—but it's all there. And the Information Age is getting bigger each and every day.

The computer has evolved from the giant mainframe to the laptop or desktop companion interacting directly with workers both at office and home. Telephone lines that once carried only voice now carry mountains of data from video applications, computers, consumer calls via toll-free telephone numbers, and fax machines. The telephone and computer have become essential business tools. Now they are joined by the facsimile machine.

The facsimile machine enables companies to be more productive, flexible, and responsive in meeting the needs of their customers. Like computers, a fax machine is cost effective, versatile, and rarely needs a day off from work. It comes as no surprise that the marriage of the three most important communication tools—the telephone, personal computer, and fax machine—generates a lot of interest, excitement, and sales.

This chapter examines the inner mysteries of connecting the PC (personal computer) to fax machines in the office and around the world. The PC-fax connection might not be for everyone, but many users find it offers the perfect combination of business communication tools.

☎ *The Complete PC offers an entire family of PC fax products that feature on-screen fax display for convenience and security. Over 100 printers and most full-page scanners are also supported. (Courtesy of The Complete PC)*

USING YOUR PC AS A FAX MACHINE

The openings or ports at the back of a desktop computer are the gateways to making a PC more productive, powerful, and flexible. Until recently, PC owners would run wires from the ports of their machines to improved monitors, to external modems linking phone lines, to image scanners, to speech and communication devices for the disabled, to cash registers, and to other noncomputer devices. Now the new buzz word, the hot item, the latest computer accessory craze isn't a board that enhances or expands computer memory—it's the *fax emulation board* or *fax modem*.

Since fax machines are generally used to communicate between remote locations, the fax emulation board gives companies increased cost-effective communications. By using PCs equipped with fax boards or fax modems, computer users can now send files to a receiving fax machine or to another PC equipped with a fax emulation board without ever touching paper or a fax machine.

A PC equipped with a fax emulation board enables a user to send memos, reports, graphics, etc. to a single fax machine or PC or broadcast to an entire network of fax machines. Via its software, the fax emulation board can dial telephone lines to fax machines or fax-equipped PCs and transmit at rates averaging 30 seconds per page. If a fax broadcast system is in place at the receiving end, copies of the same document can be delivered automatically to more than 100 fax machines or PC-fax units. Some PC-fax boards acknowledge receipt of the receiving fax right on the computer screen.

Most PC-fax boards offer "store and forward" capability. The user can specify the time of day or night the document is to be sent, and the computer will send the document automatically. Besides saving money by transmitting at off-peak hours, many users find phone lines more accessible after business hours. In addition, the PC-fax board eliminates the optical scanning step required by conventional fax units. This results in better print quality with crisper, easier-to-read text.

Most personal computer fax boards can perform *ASCII-to-fax format conversions* (converting computer information to fax form for transmission over the telephone); *broadcast* (send documents to multiple locations automatically by specifying a list of telephone numbers to call at a specific time so transmission occurs automatically); *polling* (request data from a remote, unattended station by configuring the fax card to call a designated group of fax numbers at a specified time to see if they have anything to deliver); *automatic logging* (an activity log or journal indicating fax transmission); and *automatic dialing/sending* and *answer/receiving* of transmissions.

PC-FAX APPEAL

"Image Communications" is the trendy term used to define the process of high-tech communications. Combining the computer's two most powerful selling points—graphics and communications—the marketplace is buzzing with products designed to enhance PC-fax communications.

Millions of pages of text and graphics are transmitted by fax machines every day. The fax machine user merely inserts a document into the fax machine and in 30 seconds or less, bit-mapped text and graphics emerge from a remote facsimile machine as exact duplicates of the original. This process is now easier to accomplish than ever before, and the new generation of fax machines is less expensive, more compact, more reliable, and easier to use. And, technological advances have made microcomputer fax cards as easy to use as the stand-alone fax machine while offering better image quality and the ability to store files to disk.

HOW DO I GET A
LETTER ON DISK TO LONDON?

Using the same RJ-11 telephone connectors used by standard fax machines to tie into phone lines, the computer-based facsimile transceiver board is a section or part of a stand-alone facsimile machine. Also called *fax modem cards*, a fax-equipped personal computer uses a 9,600 bps (bits per second) fax modem and related software. The modem and its software work together to convert ASCII files, screen captures, and graphics into compressed, bit-mapped images and digital information suitable for transmission as an analog signal over phone lines to other fax units. The receiving fax unit or fax-equipped personal computer converts the analog signals to digital, decompresses the image, and prints out the transmission, displays it on screen, or stores it on disk.

Documents transmitted via a fax modem have a better quality than those transmitted via a stand-alone fax machine. This is because the optical scanning step is omitted when using the fax modem. What is seen on the sender's computer screen is what the receiving PC-fax receives. Even if a PC-fax sends to a stand-alone facsimile, the resultant image is usually sharper because the optical scanning step is omitted.

The fax modem board consists of a printed circuit card that fits into a standard expansion slot found in the PC. Via accompanying software, the modem uses the 9,600 bps CCITT (Consultative Committee for International Telephone and Telegraph) standard established in 1980. All personal computer fax boards comply with the 9,600 bps transmission rate used by Group III stand-alone fax units. Some PC-fax units can even communicate with the older Group II fax machines. Group III units specify transmission rates between 30 to 60 seconds per page. Group II units specify a transmission rate of three minutes per page.

Unlike standard fax units, the fax modem does not come with a telephone but usually includes a jack to plug in a telephone. In addition, since a fax modem does not include an optical scanner or printer, manufacturers are rushing to bring these accessories to market. Accessories targeted at the "image communications" industry include scanning equipment, graphics boards, optical character recognition (OCR) software, and high-capacity-disk storage units.

THE PC-FAX ADVANTAGE

The main advantage of a fax modem over a standard fax machine is the ability to send documents as they appear on the computer screen without first having to print out the image and then load it into a fax machine. Compared to standard fax machine printouts on flimsy thermal paper, fax modem transmissions can be printed on laster printers for maximum detail on quality bond paper. Fax machines that can print on bond paper are considerably less common than are laster printers tied to computers.

Since electronic mail services generally can't handle complex graphics, the fax modem is a wise choice for those who work with graphics. Even with the Group III standard of 200 dots per inch, fax computer boards outperform the transmission quality of E-mail (electronic mail) services. However, it is difficult to edit most fax transmissions at the receiving end. Whether it's a stand-alone fax machine or a PC-fax, faxing a document helps conquer the deadline and takes a bite out of overnight courier business—all for the price of a phone call.

FAX BOARD FEATURES

Today's fax market is one of multiple alternatives: stand-alone fax machines, fax services, or PC-fax boards/modems. Like stand-alone fax units, PC-fax boards vary considerably in features. Most units have a built-in modem (some units require a separate modem). Units might have their own processor, vary in the amount of memory they are equipped with or require from the PC, and use software of varying sophistication. In addition, a hard disk is required for storing ASCII files as they are converted for transmittal or received. All PC-fax boards let users send and receive documents directly from one PC to another PC or stand-alone fax machine.

The resident modem on the fax board converts ASCII files on a PC to an image, or facsimile, format and transmits the converted data over telephone lines. These modems are considerably faster than early Group I and II fax machines, which are based on analog technology. Early Group I machines operated much like the standard 300 bps modem and took up to six minutes to transmit a single page. Group II machines cut transmission time in half, taking up to three minutes to transmit a single page. These units first appeared in the mid 1970s.

In 1980, the Consultative Committee for International Telephone and Telegraphy gave fax its first major technological thrust when it approved the 9,600 bps Group III standard. Most of today's stand-alone fax machines and fax boards conform to that standard. Group III incorporated digital image scanning and data compression methods.

The majority of Group III products, including the modems within facsimile boards, use the Rockwell V.29 chip set. This chip set uses the CCITT V.29 half-duplex 9,600 bps file transmission standard and the Modified Huffman compression scheme. The family of Rockwell chips used by Group III machines defines the standard for high-speed, dial-up facsimile transmission. The stand-alone fax machine uses the compression scheme to compress much of the white space in a document. (Compression can be observed when the fax machine is scanning a document with lots of white space. The machine moves past the white space and slows down only when the scanner encounters an image area.) The fax image file is *compressed* (encoded) en route to the remote machine; once it arrives, it is *decompressed* (decoded) for printing or storage to disk. (Note: Some fax boards are capable of talking with older Group II machines.)

As with standard modems, the speed at which the fax modem operates is the determining factor of cost and applicability of a fax board. The best resolution found on Group III fax machines is about 200 dots per inch. In normal transmission mode on a "clean" phone line, it takes from 15 to 20 seconds to transmit a standard page of 203 pixels per horizontal inch by 98 lines per inch. When transmitting pages with lots of graphics, transmission takes place in fine mode. Fine mode increases vertical resolution to 196 lines per inch. However, this doubles transmission time and increases transmission costs. Also, adding the gray scale provides higher resolution while slowing down transmission.

Group III fax transmission occurs at the standard rate of 9,600 bps. However, if a fax machine is sending to a slower Group II machine, it will "fall back" and transmit at 7,200 bps, or 4,800 bps. *Fallback* or *dropback* also occurs if a machine is unable to make a connection at 9,600 bps. Fallback slows down transmission, but the improved transmission quality and convenience outweigh the extra time and expense.

The difference between standard computer-to-computer communication and fax-to-fax communication is that fax machines don't use any error-checking protocols. This makes fax communications faster by maximizing throughput, but it makes transmissions susceptible to small holes in the image—those small white dots often seen in the printouts. Fortunately, these "data hits" aren't critical to the image—the loss is minimal and acceptable. Data hits are critical, however, to certain types of data such as computer program information. (Note: Some fax machines do utilize an error-correction scheme but don't eliminate data hits.)

When the new Group IV fax machines become available, transmissions will take place at the rate of 30 pages per minute.

☎ *Computer Friends offers this full-featured fax board. The board has an RJ-11 jack for connecting a telephone. (Courtesy of Computer Friends)*

Group IV machines require the use of digital telephone lines or Integrated Services Digital Network. In the meantime, Rockwell has introduced the new CMOS, low-power, full-duplex V.32 9,600 bps (modem on a chip) modem board. This advance allows fax cards to support full-duplex fax or modem transmission at 9,600 bps.

BACKGROUND OPERATION

Background operation is advertised by many fax modem manufacturers. This means the fax board and software perform their tasks without interfering or interrupting a foreground operation (word processing, for example). However, most fax boards pause the foreground operation when a fax transmission is received or when the user wants to send a fax document. Manufacturers commonly refer to this pause as "terminate-and-stay-resident" or "quasi-background" operation.

Background operation is certainly desirable, but true background operation requires the fax board to be equipped with an on-board microprocessor and its own memory or RAM. The fax board coprocessor off-loads fax-related processing from the personal computer's processor and enables fax transmissions to occur without slowing down or interrupting the foreground application.

The personal computer provides the capabilities for storage of digitized documents to disk, and the software enables fax board manufacturers to incorporate more enhanced features than are possible with stand-alone fax machines. For optimum performance, the fax board requires that the personal computer have a processor that is faster than the original IBM/XT's 4.77 MHz. This enables the processor-equipped fax card to operate in the background. The faster processor won't speed up actual transmission time but will accelerate text file to fax format (and vice versa) conversion time. A hard disk is necessary to store and manipulate the files generated by and for fax transmission.

A fax board doesn't require any larger memory than the DOS 640K and does not make use of numeric coprocessors. Fax boards work well with standard video display adapters: color graphics adapter, enhanced graphics adapter, and video graphics adapter types originated by IBM, plus common high-resolution monochrome display drivers.

SOFTWARE

The software that accompanies a fax board enables the board and host PC to perform the various fax functions: facsimile file management, storage of telephone numbers, and, very important, the conversion of nonfacsimile files (such as documents generated with desktop publishing software) to facsimile format. Hopefully, conversion will retain the original file's form, typeface(s), and content. The key issue is whether the fax board's software includes a graphics, or image, editor. An easy-to-use integral graphics editor eliminates the need to buy an extra package.

Besides converting files for transmission and editing, the software should enable facsimile boards to produce hard copy on most common printers. Because facsimiles contain more than just text, the printers must be driven in graphics mode (eliminating daisywheel-type printers and dot-matrix printers, which do not operate in a graphics mode). Most of the fax boards support printers by Epson and Toshiba and most of the popular laser printers.

The most common fax board software enables the boards to function much the same as stand-alone fax machines. The software manages the storage, reception, and transmission of files. Transmission programs control whether and how many times transmission should be attempted when an attempt fails, such as how many times to retry a busy number. Transmission and reception programs can operate "in the background." This enables a fax board to receive or send transmissions while the computer is being used for other tasks such as word processing.

Lists of recipients and corresponding messages are also managed by software. Lists that direct a single facsimile message to many recipients, several facsimiles to a single recipient, or groups of documents to various recipients are all controlled and generated via the appropriate software. Some software enables certain fax boards to accept and relay messages to other units and even interact with voice-messaging services.

The same software generates the transmission log, which indicates incoming as well as outgoing transmissions, the called or calling parties, call durations, etc. In addition, as with most stand-alone machines, the software can print out a report when transmission difficulties occur such as line fail, busy, or no carrier.

Accompanying software can make all the difference in the functionality of a PC-fax board. Because manufacturers are constantly developing newer, more powerful applications software for their fax boards, we can be assured of more powerful and sophisticated fax board packages. However, whatever PC-fax board manufacturers develop, most of the functions will be performed by the software—Group III fax machine standards will not be affected by fax board developments. Therefore, you can be readily assured that a fax board compatible with Group III standards will change only through the software that drives it and the host PC.

PC-FAX ACCESSORIES

A basic PC-fax system might include just the fax modem board and a host computer complete with printer. Although such a configuration might be the most common one, many fax users will have or will want to add other equipment to round out their systems.

Manufacturers apparently agree and have begun to market accessories directed to the PC-fax user. Currently, manufacturers are emphasizing image scanners and voice-mail boards.

Image Scanners

To be most functional, the PC-fax board should be able to get a printed sheet of information into the host computer's memory in facsimile format. This enables the PC operator to manipulate and work with the document on his/her computer's screen. Some fax cards include special optical-character-recognition (OCR) software for this purpose. OCR technology combines a scanner with software that recognizes characters and turns a scanned piece of text into a word-processing or other document. Many fax cards include a port to connect a scanner directly to the fax card.

Because not all fax cards are compatible with every graphics format, text and graphics editing capabilities can be very important to the user. It is helpful if the conversion software supports the TIFF (Tag Image File Format) if you use PageMaker, .PCX files for Paintbrush, etc. Note that some scanners can produce an image at a higher resolution than the Group III fax is capable of handling. Such scanners come with software that converts image data into one or more interchange formats, thus making the files suitable for facsimile transmission via the software used by the fax board. A related feature is the ability to handle gray-scale images. Gray scale is most important when transmitting photographs and/or multicolor or shaded drawings.

☎ *The LightScan 200 is a popular hand-held image scanner. (Courtesy of Computer Friends)*

Voice Mail

A voice-mail device turns a PC into an answering machine. The device enables the PC to play messages, record incoming audio messages, and control and initiate various programs via dial-tone signals.

Applications for voice messaging include selling services, sales prospecting, follow-up selling, and providing information to clients. Many companies have found that voice mail helps eliminate telephone tag and improves message communication between and among staff members. For the consumer, such a device can be used to order products with a touch-tone phone and to control everything from home appliances to security systems—all from a remote PC or even an ordinary telephone.

CD-ROM and Fax

Libraries, businesses, and government agencies are exploring the power and flexibility of CD-ROM. They use CD-ROM data-

bases networked with fax machines and fax modems to share huge
reference resources. This enables remote offices via fax machines
to receive and request searches from source libraries. PC-fax software is used by source libraries to enable them to transmit search
results directly from the computer and disc player running the CD-
ROM database to the requesting party's fax machine or fax-board-
equipped PC. Such technology enables research-dependent companies, offices, and government agencies to respond and operate in
a more timely and cost efficient manner—immediate reference services via the fax.

FAX BOARD/MODEM MARKETPLACE

A fax board can be placed into one of three categories as identified by the functions it is capable of performing.

✤ *Low-end* PC-fax boards are basically just on-board modems that
eat up computer memory and the PC's processing power. They
can do little more than send and receive fax transmissions.
✤ *Intelligent* fax boards are equipped with a modem, a microprocessor, memory, and software. Unlike low-end boards, intelligent boards allow fax transmission to take place in the background while the computer continues to be used for other tasks.
The fax board provides the coprocessor and memory necessary
for such background operations to take place.
✤ *Integrated Intelligent* fax boards are integrated with third-party
software and can serve network and multiple workstations on a
LAN (local area network).

Most stand-alone and network-based fax boards support DOS
and can transmit at speeds of 9,600, 7,200, 4,800, or 2,400 bits per
second. These transmission speeds support the CCITT, Group III
facsimile format and coding standard. The Group III standards
specify that equipment transmit a letter-size page in less than one
minute over voice-grade telephone lines.

PC-FAX COMPARISON CHART

The PC-Fax Comparison Chart will help you select the PC-fax
board that best meets your needs. Although manufacturers offer an
array of features with various fax cards, you should keep in mind
how you will actually use the card. You should analyze the price of

the fax board to see if its benefits and add-on costs (PC, hard disk, printer, scanner, etc.) outweigh the purchase of a stand-alone fax machine.

Since the fax board marketplace is evolving at a fast pace, buyers are advised to check with the manufacturer or retail dealer for the most current product specifications. See Appendix A for PC-fax board manufacturers' names and addresses. (Fax modems and fax-related software and accessories for the Apple Macintosh computer are listed separately within Appendix A.)

PC–Fax Board Comparison Chart			
Product/Manufacturer			
List Price			
Auto-dial/ sending			
Auto-answer/ receiving			
Broadcasting			
Polling			
High-speed nonfax file transfers			
Background operation			
Fax-compatible image compression			
Fax-compatible image storage on disk			
Standard files converted			
Built-in OCR capabilities			
Built-in Scanner capabilities			
On-screen preview			
Image Editing capabilities			
Gray Scale capabilities			
Printers Supported			
Phone Book			
Page size			
Software Features			
Warranty			

MACINTOSH FAX MODEMS

Since the Macintosh is a graphics-based computer capable of creating high-resolution images, it is listed separately from other personal computers. Its unique user interface and wide use in desktop publishing make the Mac an ideal candidate for fax communications. This section looks briefly at three fax modems for the Mac. Additional fax-related software and image scanners for the Macintosh are listed in Appendix A.

AppleFax Modem

Apple Computer's special-purpose AppleFax Modem is designed to communicate with Group III fax machines and other AppleFax stations; it is not usable as a stand-alone modem unless you are communicating with another AppleFax. The unit has an external port onto which peripherals such as a modem or printer can be connected. A pass-through switch on its front panel lets you use a regular modem for telecommunicating without disconnecting the AppleFax.

Installation is easy. The fax modem is connected to a standard phone outlet with the provided cable and to the Mac's modem port via an Apple System Peripheral-8 Cable (not included). An RJ-11 jack on the back panel of the AppleFax modem enables the user to connect a telephone.

To transmit a fax document, Apple provides a resource that is installed in the System Folder. Once installed, the user merely selects the fax resource from the Chooser while using the word processor, for example. When the program's print command is issued, the working file is converted to fax format and can be sent to any fax number. Any program that uses the standard print command can be used to create and send a fax document. Both text and graphics can be sent—not just text.

A fax document also can be sent via the AppleFax application. This uses address books to store the names and numbers of fax stations. Other features provided by the AppleFax application include: immediate transmission or transmission at an appointed time, transmission to an intermediate or holding AppleFax station for later forwarding to other stations, sending multiple files to one location or the same files to multiple locations, and generation of activity or transmission reports. In addition, you can view and print fax transmissions.

To receive a fax transmission, first turn on the modem, followed by the start up of the AppleFax application. The modem then remains in "wait for call mode." Background operation is not possible with the software as supplied by Apple. However, BackFax from Solutions International enables the AppleFax modem to operate in the background. The Mac can then be used for other applications such as word processing while receiving and sending fax transmissions.

Since the Macintosh is known for its array of fonts, the AppleFax modem offers four letter-quality fonts in a variety of point sizes for creating fax documents. This is especially useful for those needing to fax page layout documents.

Abaton Inter-Fax

The Abaton Inter-Fax 24/96 is a 9,600 bps, MMP Level 5, Group III fax modem and a 1,200 bps Hayes-compatible data modem. Physically the unit is similar to a desktop modem that is designed to sit under a standard telephone. The unit has nine LEDs on the front panel to inform the user of modem activities. The unit is shipped ready-to-use with fax software and cables for connecting to the back of a Macintosh and to a telephone line.

☎ *Abaton's InterFax 24/96 combines a 2,400 bps MMP5 data modem with a 9,600 bps fax modem, which allows the user to send and receive multiple fax documents from within Macintosh applications. The InterFax also works "in the background" with or without Multi-Finder. (Courtesy of Abaton)*

FAXstf

This is a portable modem from STF Techologies. The unit includes a small power supply, cables, and software. The unit cannot be used as a regular data modem.

MacFax

MacFax gives the Macintosh both fax and data modem capabilities. This compact unit can send and receive facsimiles from any Group II or Group III fax, connecting the user to virtually any installed fax machine around the world. Orchid Technology has loaded this product with features even the most demanding fax user can appreciate: scanner support, electronic inbox/outbox to monitor fax documents, group dial capabilities, and other powerful features.

PC-FAX BOARDS—NO SUBSTITUTE FOR THE STAND-ALONE FAX

The PC-fax board is intended to complement, not replace, the stand-alone fax machine. Fax machines are easy to use, unlike the average PC that requires many hours of training. Most importantly, as stand-alone fax units prices continue to fall, many individuals might still find that the PC and its required accessories—scanner, hard disk, laser printer, etc.—make the stand-alone fax most efficient and applicable to their needs.

Whether your needs and/or budget dictate a stand-alone or PC-fax capabilities, Chapter Nine offers useful ideas on ways to put the power of fax to work for you.

CHAPTER NINE

Putting the Fax to Work

THE FAX MACHINE PROVIDES A WAY TO COMMUNICATE WORLD-wide almost instantly. The technology is affordable, easy to use, and reliable. In addition, today's fax machines offer an array of features that enable them to operate unattended, alert the user of transmission difficulties, and even keep track of calls and other information.

The powerful and multitalented fax has proven its worth to those who work at home as well as those who commute to an office. To many individuals, fax has given them the freedom to modify work hours, work location(s), and even basic work philosophies. No longer tied to a set office routine, the fax is being put to work by those who see its potential to help them meet ever-increasing work loads, accommodate the need for more flexibility in the hours of business operations, and be more effective in overall communications.

WAYS FOR FAX TO HELP YOU

Fax technology is only as good as the benefits the user derives from its use. While some consider the fax a godsend; others consider it an intrusive tool used by impatient, demanding managers to keep track of them. Whether good or bad, managers, businesses, and individuals from giant corporations to mom-and-pop delicatessens are finding fax to be a friend.

**"...Sure! Uh, hold on Mr. Smith. I can FAX it right to you!
I'll be in in the morning if you have any questions!"**

The most important question to ask before incorporating the use of a fax into a business is "How can fax help my business?" There are many proven ways fax has helped many businesses, but each business and fax application is unique. Examples of ways fax machines can help you are:

❖ Send shipping notices to expedite customer billing.
❖ Notify plant/branch supervisors.
❖ Send revisions to contracts, plans, etc.
❖ Receive delicatessen orders from customers via fax machines.
❖ Relay sales orders instantly from conventions, sales meetings, satellite offices, or from a vehicle via a cellular car phone.
❖ Inform purchasing departments when inventories are low.
❖ Get purchase orders to vendors.
❖ Revise advertising/newsletter copy.
❖ Expedite transfer of contracts and legal documents. (Note: Signatures on faxed documents are considered legally binding.)
❖ Send press releases.
❖ Speedy transfer of payroll/time cards.
❖ Send credit applications and receive approvals.
❖ Process insurance forms.

✤ Children can keep in contact with teachers/classmates while recuperating at home.
✤ Make investments; send orders/authorizations instantly.
✤ Send and receive detailed charts, drawings, forms, or design specifications.
✤ Send and receive quotations and bids.
✤ Obtain confirmation of information received by using automatic status reports that let the sender know documents were received.
✤ Improve office communications.
✤ Reduce clerical staff time by sending documents to multiple locations automatically.
✤ Reduce long-distance telephone charges by sending documents unattended when rates are lowest.
✤ Send and receive training rosters.

☎ *Dr. Michael Roth uses a fax machine to send patient records to another dental office. Medical records can be transmitted to doctors across the country within minutes.*

☎ *Justin uses a fax machine to participate in classroom instruction while he is recuperating at home. Here Justin is faxing a completed assignment to his teacher.*

☎ *After Justin's teacher checks his work, the next assignment is faxed to him. The fax machine lets Justin work on assignments along with other students in the classroom.*

THE COMPETITIVE EDGE

The fax machine has made businesses more competitive while improving overall communications. Some businesses are even participating in a form of cooperative advertising. By using a master order form for product/service information, vendors list their individual fax numbers to which customers can fax requests for product/service information. Vendors can then either fax, mail, or call prospective clients/customers while customer interest level is high. Such a response to customer inquiries can increase sales dramatically.

Fax might well prove to be one of the best marketing tools of modern business. Its power is readily available, even when on the road. Faxit Corporation has been placing credit-card-activated public facsimile systems in airports, hotels, and other busy locations throughout the United States. Even the traveler can stay in touch with home or office and conduct business without being there.

Fax definitely provides an edge in today's highly competitive marketplace. With the need for instananeous communications becoming greater each and every day, fax is the one solution many businesses cannot do without.

SAY IT WRITE

The power of fax communications has created a problem for those who generate the documents being faxed. The problem is the perceived lack of time for editing documents; if it's going to be faxed, it must be a priority. In meeting the demand for "right now" communications, fax users are sending documents faster and in greater volume than ever before. The demand for near instantaneous document delivery means that increased pressure is applied to those who conceive and create printed materials: advertisements, brochures, scripts, etc. Now, Franklin Computer has a line of writing tools that can help even the seasoned author meet those tight deadlines.

Franklin offers a line of hand-held electronic reference products. Easy to use, compact, and powerful, these user friendly computers can check spelling, supply words from a thesaurus, provide complete definitions, and even amuse you with built-in games while you wait in the line at the fax machine. When you need to say it right, Franklin will help you write it.

Chapter Ten can help you keep your fax in top working order. In addition, the chapter offers a troubleshooting section to help solve common fax malfunctions.

☎ *Unlike other public fax services that require staffing or time-consuming instructions and maintenance, FAXIT offers a simple-to-use, cost-effective system that utilizes three basic components: a Group III fax machine, a public telephone, and a credit card swipe reader. (Courtesy of FAXIT Corporation)*

☎ *Franklin Computer's Language Master 4000 (LM-4000) is the world's only electronic dictionary, thesaurus, and phonetic spelling corrector and word game player that pronounces over 83,000 words. The Language Master 4000 provides more than 274,000 definitions, 487,000 synonyms, and phonetic spelling and speech for more than 83,000 words. Franklin offers an entire line of electronic reference tools. (Courtesy of Franklin Computer)*

CHAPTER TEN

Fax Maintenance and Troubleshooting

FAX MACHINES ARE DESIGNED TO WITHSTAND YEARS OF HEAVY use, and they have proven themselves with impressive service records. However, even with the best machines, problems can sometimes occur. This chapter is intended to help the fax user deal with the most common problems encountered when receiving and/ or sending documents. In addition, it explains basic maintenance procedures, offers troubleshooting hints, and explains the most common fax error messages.

READ THE INSTRUCTIONS

Since fax machines are so easy to operate, there is a general trend to just plug them in, connect the telephone cord and start faxing. Although many units are that easy to use, more sophisticated full-featured units require a thorough reading of the operating instructions before attempting to operate them.

Not only will you become more aware of the features found on your fax machine, reading the manual also provides a mental checklist as to how to better use the machine. Adherence to the manufacturer's operating instructions helps ensure optimal machine performance and assures warranty coverage (improperly operating or connecting a fax machine could void the machine's factory warranty).

GET TO KNOW THE MACHINE

From the time you take the unit out of the shipping carton, you should familiarize yourself with every control, feature, and instruction for sending/receiving and copying documents. Be sure to read how to use such capabilities as Speed Dial, Coded Speed Dial, and other programmed operations. Take notes and list the steps necessary for successful fax transmission. Post instructions near the machine for handy reference.

CARING FOR YOUR FAX

In conjunction with the Fax Care Company, Buyers Laboratory, Inc. has identified the five most common evils of a fax machine to be:

✤ Inadequate ac power supply, including poor or no grounding; line noise generated by external motors or compressors on the same circuit; and recurring power spikes or brownouts.

✤ Poor-quality thermal paper resulting in poor image quality, premature fading of images and potentially damaging paper residues left on internal mechanisms.

✤ Poor or untrained fax machine operators.

✤ No preventive maintenance performed on the machine. Rarely does a fax salesperson mention that there is a need to perform periodic cleaning of such items as paper-feed mechanisms, the scanner, and the thermal print head. Few owner's manuals caution operators to keep loose paper clips and staples away from the machine or to purchase a phone and ac line surge protector for their machine.

✤ Poor-quality phone lines or lines with special features such as call waiting. Such features can cause fax transmission errors.

Singularly, any one of the above could interrupt a crucial fax communication and force the need for another, sometimes costly, phone call to complete an important transmittal. A combination of any one of the five can cripple a fax for hours or even days, costing a business not only lost time, but even worse, lost business opportunities.

CLEANING THE OUTER CASE

To remove smudges, dust, and dirt from the outer casing of a fax machine, lightly wipe the unit with a soft cloth moistened with

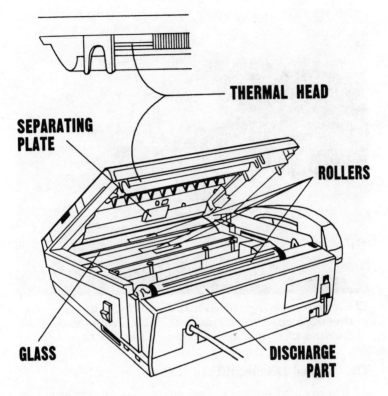

THERMAL HEAD

SEPARATING PLATE

ROLLERS

GLASS

DISCHARGE PART

☎ *A look under the cover of a typical fax machine reveals the integral components.*

water or a diluted dish-detergent solution. To prevent discoloration and malfunctions, never use thinner, benzene, alcohol or other inorganic solvents. Cleaning the inside components, rollers, etc., requires specially designed accessories.

ENTER THE FAX CARE KIT

The Fax Care Company of Deerfield, IL has specially designed their Fax Care Kits to clean the only moving parts on a fax machine, the paper-feed mechanisms, and the stationary thermal print head. The Fax Care Company staff has shared their expertise in keeping fax machines in good working order.

There are two types of paper-feed rollers on a fax, and each requires careful regular cleaning. They are the original document feed rollers and the paper supply feed rollers.

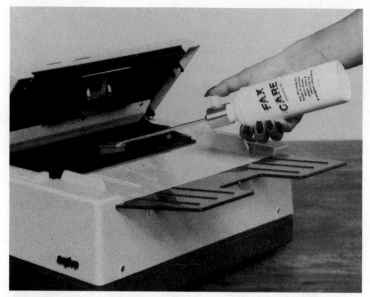

☎ *It is important to keep the original document feed rollers clean. Anything that is on the original can come off and cause transmission difficulties and/or paper jams. (Courtesy of Fax Care Company)*

The Original Document Feed Rollers

On most fax machines, there are two sets of document feed rollers that guide the paper through the paper-feed path: upper and lower. Anything that is on the document can come off as it is fed into a fax machine document feeder. This includes, but is certainly not limited to

❖ pen inks
❖ pencil leads
❖ copier toner
❖ paper dust
❖ liquid paper

As documents are fed into the fax machine, minute particles are left on the paper feed rollers.

The Paper Supply Feed Rollers

As a fax transmission is being received and printed onto the paper supply, the feed rollers that guide the transmittal out of the machine are exposed to

❖ paper dust from the paper supply itself
❖ paper coating residues

As with the original document feed rollers, minute particles are deposited on the feed rollers that come in contact with the paper supply. In addition, paper coatings can rub off onto the paper-supply feed rollers.

The Effects of Dirty Feed Rollers

Dirty rollers can result in interrupted transmission due to paper jams, original document scarring, and document misfeeds.

Interrupted Transmissions. Continuous residue buildup on feed rollers eventually causes an original document to misfeed and subsequently creates a jam in the paper path. Most fax machines

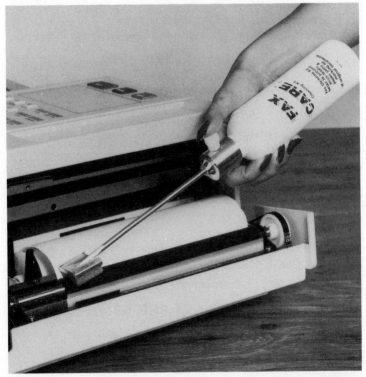

☎ *The paper-supply rollers must be kept clean if documents are to print with optimal clarity. Dirty rollers can cause paper jams, streaks, etc. (Courtesy of Fax Care Company)*

are designed to automatically disconnect the telephone connection whenever they sense a malfunction occurring in any part of the paper path areas.

Original Scarring. Excessive residue buildup on feed rollers can scar the originals in two ways:

✤ Transpose a streak or blotch onto the original. This scar is also transmitted with the other images on the original.
✤ A tear or rip can occur on the original while being fed through the machine.

Document Misfeeds. Excessive buildups on feed rollers cause poor roller traction, which results in slipping or sidetracking in paper paths. Additionally, poor roller traction can allow several documents stacked in the document feeder to feed through at the same time.

The Results of Dirty Feed Rollers

Dirty feed rollers can result in a number of fax difficulties, such as:

✤ Unnecessary downtime due to paper jams.
✤ Service calls to clear paper paths, replace failed scanner or printer parts, replace failed power supplies, or replace failed modems.
✤ Wasted time, energy and money spent resending interrupted transmittals.
✤ Increased traffic at fax machine due to resending of documents.
✤ Reduced confidence in the fax machine's dependability.
✤ Reduced confidence in and increased tensions between the fax vendor and the fax owner.
✤ Reduced image clarity of transmissions received.
✤ Reduced image clarity of documents sent.

HOW TO USE THE FAX CARE KIT

The Fax Care Company makes fax machine care easy with their Fax Care Kits designed specifically to clean all machine feed rollers that can be accessed easily, in addition to the thermal print head. Unlike other cleaning kits that are designed for computer use and labeled for fax machine use, The Fax Care Kit is designed specifically to meet the unique cleaning needs of fax machines. These kits do so with no abrasive chemicals.

Fax Care recommends weekly cleaning of a machine that receives moderate to heavy use. Daily cleaning is recommended for machines that receive heavy use.

The kit comes with one 6-ounce bottle of cleaning solution with a reusable storage cap, an applicator system consisting of an applicator holder assembly and flow plunger, three foam applicator pads, and special wipes for cleaning the exterior of the fax machine. The system is easy to use:

1) Attach the applicator to the cleaning solution bottle.
2) Locate the original document feed rollers.
3) Invert the bottle and push the plunger until the applicator pad is slightly moist.
4) Press the pad against the rollers and begin rubbing pad side-to-side while manually turning the roller until all of the roller surface has been cleaned thoroughly.

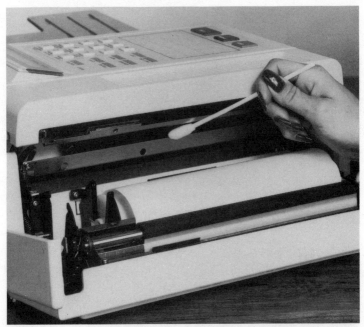

☎ *The thermal print head is often neglected by fax machine operators. Dirt and residue buildups can render fax printouts illegible. (Courtesy of Fax Care Company)*

5) Repeat steps 3 and 4 on the paper-supply feed rollers.
6) Clean the thermal print head with the special cleaning swabs supplied with the Fax Care Kit.

After cleaning has been accomplished, dispose of the foam pad, remove applicator system from bottle, put the bottle cap onto the solution bottle, and store all items in the storage container. (The solutions are nonabrasive, nonstaining, nonflammable, nondiscoloring, nonconductive, noncorrosive, and odorless.)

SURGE PROTECTION

Fax machines, like other solid-state or microprocessor-based equipment, are sensitive to changes in power and telephone lines: voltage drops, surges, spikes, and electronic noise from appliances such as air conditioners. Many personal computer users have seen their computers destroyed or severely damaged by spikes in both ac power lines and through phone line/modem connections (lightning is a frequent culprit). Fax machines are equally as sensitive to such occurrences.

Ac power line surges can cause severe, immediate damage as

☎ *The Ruby Plus and Diamond Plus surge protectors offer enhanced protection for sensitive electronic and communications equipment. (Courtesy of Curtis Manufacturing Company, Inc.)*

well as shorten equipment life. Additionally, damage to computers and peripheral hardware (fax machines, too) can occur in the form of erroneous data output or data loss. In fact, ac power line surges, typically 1,000 volts or more, occur an average of 100 times per month per household.

Connection errors and loss of carrier, numerous reconnects, loss of fax memory or programming, and other transmission difficulties could be indicative of electrical power disturbances present on phone or electric lines. To prevent transmission difficulties caused by power disturbances and prolong the useful life of a fax machine, both telephone and ac power line connections should be protected.

Curtis Manufacturing Company, Inc. offers an array of accessories that provide electronic surge protection specially designed to protect valuable telephone communications equipment. Curtis' phone line surge protection helps prevent damage to sensitive equipment such as fax, telex, telephones, modems, etc. from dangerous high-voltage surges. These surge protectors "clamp" harmful power surges, controlling the amount of voltage that can pass through to facsimile, modem, and telephone lines, thereby protecting sensitive computer and electronic equipment from internal damage.

Curtis offers an entire line of electronic surge protection accessories. Don't forget VCRs, stereo equipment, and other valuable sensitive electronic equipment—Curtis has the solution to any surge protection problem at home or at the office. When selecting any surge protector, be sure to look for a UL 1449 listing (Underwriter's Laboratory). Surge protectors used for telecommunications equipment should carry a UL 497A listing.

FAX PAPER

Each fax machine has been designed to achieve optimal performance when used properly. Besides understanding how to operate and care for a fax machine, the user needs to use the correct paper in the machine. The correct paper means using paper that meets the manufacturer's specifications and is the correct size roll. The owner's manual should indicate the proper coated stock to use in the machine. Because paper varies widely in quality and image reproduction quality, follow the manufacturer's recommendations. The use of the proper paper in the machine is critical.

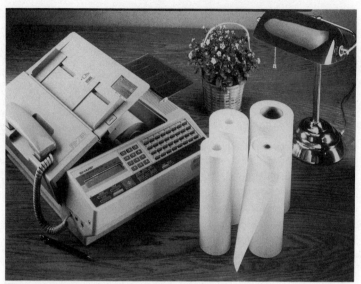

☎ *Fax machine paper rolls come in various sizes and can vary widely in quality. Be sure to purchase paper that meets the manufacturer specifications for your machine. (Courtesy of Demco, Inc.)*

Fax machine paper usually has an expiration date stamped on the packaging. Do not use paper that has exceeded the expiration date. The use of only fresh paper will help ensure optimal machine performance and better image quality.

Storing Paper

Paper should be stored in a cool, dark, and moisture-proof location, preferably in the original bag. Paper stored for long periods of time tends to curl excessively and is difficult to use. Exposure to excessive heat, such as in an automobile during the summer, can render an entire paper supply useless because the paper will turn completely black.

FAX CARE RULES

Fax machines are durable, dependable, and require adherence to just a few rules for care and maintenance.

❖ Follow owner's manual guidelines.
❖ Don't expose a fax machine to direct sunlight, extreme changes in temperature, dust, or dirt.

❖ Use the correct paper, store paper properly, and don't use paper that exceeds the expiration date stamped on the carton.

❖ Always turn the machine off before replacing the paper roll. If you don't, you might experience error messages such as replace roll or paper misfeed.

❖ Remove staples, paper clips, rubber bands, etc., from all papers before placing them in the fax unit. These items can cause severe damage to the machine's rollers and/or scanner, resulting in transmission errors, paper jams, and torn original documents.

❖ Do not use correction fluid or tape on documents to be faxed. If you must use them, make a copy of the original and fax the copy.

❖ Should a document jam inside the machine during transmission, don't attempt to pull it out. Press Stop before attempting to clear the paper path. Likewise, do not pull paper out of the machine when receiving a transmission. Always wait for the machine to stop or let the automatic paper cutter do its job.

TROUBLESHOOTING

Since fax machines receive and transmit documents, most difficulties arise either when attempting to receive and print documents or when trying to send them. This section lists typical fax machine problems and common solutions to the problems.

Document Does Not Feed Into the Machine

If the document does not feed into the machine properly, it might not have been properly inserted into the document holder. As a result, the document might not be pulled into the machine, or it might feed at an angle and cause a paper jam. Press Stop and try refeeding the document.

Clearing Recording Paper Jams

Before trying to clear recording paper jams, turn the machine's power off. This usually erases any documents received in the machine's memory and also erases the settings for sending at a preset time. If there are documents in the memory, you will have to contact the party who sent them and have them try sending again after you clear the jam. If there is a time setting for sending at a preset time, reset the time after clearing the jam.

❖ Turn the power off.
❖ Open the recording paper cover.
❖ Remove the jammed paper and reload the recording paper.
❖ Close the recording paper cover.
❖ Use the machine's copy feature to check printing operations.

To prevent the paper from stacking or jamming as it exits the machine, place the unit so the paper can fall clear of the machine. This is especially important when many or multipage documents are received.

Streaks and Dirty Patterns on Papers

If a streak or dirty pattern appears on your copy or transmitted document, clean the paper rollers, the glass window of the scanner, and/or the thermal print head. When a document cannot be fed into the unit even after repeated tries, clean the separating plate and rollers. (To clean rollers, etc., see instructions for fax maintenance above.)

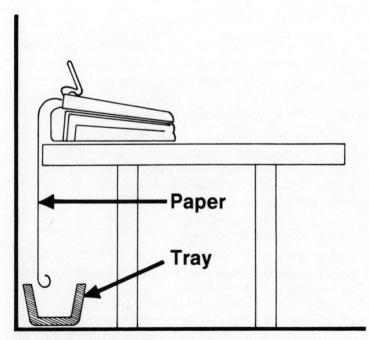

Paper

Tray

☎ *In order to prevent paper jams and pile-ups, be sure paper can fall clear of obstacles as it exits the fax machine.*

Scratchy Recording Image

A recording image that is scratched and cannot be read is usually due to the sender transmitting a light-density document. Have the sender darken the density of a document (e.g. by copying) and transmit it again.

Telephone Line Connection Difficulties

The following situations can cause a fax communication to be aborted or to have distorted characters.

❖ If the telephone line is equipped with a call waiting service and a second call is received.
❖ If a telephone that is connected in parallel to the machine is picked up.
❖ If the receiving machine is not set to fax or automatic mode.
❖ If the receiving machine is out of paper.
❖ If receiving documents for a long time, the unit could overheat, stop printing, and terminate the call until the unit cools down.

When using an automatic dialer, be sure the fax number has been stored into the fax memory. Most machines can automatically select a fax memory station when a document is placed in the unit.

When receiving or making a copy of a document whose background is very dark or contains photographs, some fax machines might produce a high tone (this is normal).

Unable to Receive Documents Manually

If you are unable to receive a document in manual mode, make sure that

❖ you haven't fed a document into the fax unit.
❖ you press Start before hanging up the receiver.
❖ there is no document received in the unit's memory.

Unable to Poll Other Units

If a fax is unable to poll other units, make sure that

❖ you haven't fed a document into the fax machine.
❖ polling IDs match.
❖ there is recording paper in the unit.

❖ the other party has set their fax unit to receive documents automatically.

❖ the other party has properly fed a document into their unit.

❖ you dial the other party's number from the handset.

The Fax Won't Make Copies

If a fax won't make copies, be sure the receiver is on the hook.

The Fax is Unable to Send
Documents through Relay Units

If your fax has the capability to send documents through relay units, be sure that

❖ your fax number is registered with your unit.

❖ your fax number is registered with the relay unit.

❖ the receiving units (final destinations) are registered with the relay units.

The Fax Unit Can't Send Confidential Documents

If the fax unit can't send confidential documents, make sure that

❖ the confidential mailbox number you registered in your unit matches that of the other party.

❖ the other party has registered the confidential mailbox to which you are sending.

The Fax Does Nothing

If the fax machine does nothing,

❖ the unit might have overheated and shut itself down. Let it cool.

❖ make sure the power switch is turned on.

❖ make sure the power plug is firmly plugged in.

When All Else Fails

If none of the suggestions correct the problem, turn the power off. Wait three seconds and turn it on again. Then try the procedure again.

Sometimes the problem is due to the other party's facsimile unit. If you are sure that your unit is working properly, have the other party check their unit. Make sure that the unit you are trying to communicate with is compatible with your fax unit.

WARRANTY SERVICE AND/OR REPAIR

Fax machines have proven themselves reliable. Yet, not even periodic maintenance and strict adherence to operating instructions can prevent unforeseen repairs.

Most fax users become very dependent on their fax machine, and they are shocked when it suddenly needs service or repair. Therefore, the availability of fax repair and service should be considered when the machine is purchased or leased—not when an unexpected equipment breakdown sends the fax owner scurrying to find a repair facility.

Some manufacturers offer convenient service centers, and others can diagnose and correct many minor difficulties right over the telephone via specially designed fax diagnostic equipment. Ask about turnaround time and the possibility of a loaner or the availability of a rental unit until your fax machine is repaired.

To prevent unnecessary service calls and/or equipment malfunctions, keep the fax owner's manual and service center repair numbers readily available. Before calling for service, be sure to follow the troubleshooting tips mentioned above and in your fax machine owner's manual. If you can't solve the problem, contact your local authorized service facility.

APPENDIX A

Fax Machine, Modem, and Software Manufacturers

THE GROWTH IN FAX MACHINE SALES HAS SEEN A NUMBER OF companies join the fax bandwagon. The newest products to join the fax marketplace are fax modems. These modems enable PCs to communicate with fax machines and other similarly equipped PCs without the usual complexities encountered when communicating with a PC.

This appendix offers a listing of fax machine and fax modem manufacturers as well as suppliers of computer software useful to the fax user. Products specific to the Apple Macintosh computer are listed separately in this appendix.

FAX MACHINE MANUFACTURERS

Adler-Royal Business Machines
1600 Route 22, P.O. Box 1597
Union, NJ 07083

Alden Electronics
40 Washington Street
Westborough, MA 01581-0500

AT&T
Parsippany, NJ 07054

Avatex, Inc.
1230 Oakmead Parkway
Sunnyvale, CA 94086

Brother International Corporation
Piscataway, NJ 08854

Canon, U.S.A., Inc.
One Canon Plaza
Lake Success, NY 11042
(516)488-6700

Cobra
Dynascan Corporation
6500 West Cortland Street
Chicago, IL 60635

Executone Information Systems, Inc.
6 Thorndal Circle
Darien, CT 06820

Fujitsu Imaging Systems of America, Inc.
Corporate Drive
Danbury, CT 06810

Gestetner Corporation
Gestetner Park
Yonkers, NY 10703

Harris (3M)
2300 Parklake Drive, NE
Atlanta, GA 30345-2979

Hitachi America, Ltd.
Norcross, GA 30093

Iwatsu America, Inc.
430 Commerce Boulevard
Carlstadt, NJ 07072
(201)935-8580

Konica Business Machines USA, Inc.
500 Day Hill Road
Windsor, CT 06095

Lanier Voice Products Division
1700 Chantilly Drive, NE
Atlanta, GA 30324

Minolta
101 Williams Drive
Ramsey, NJ 07446
(800)821-7700 ext. 327

Mita
Mita Copystar America, Inc.
P.O. Box 599
Paterson, NJ 07424
(800)222-6482

Mitsubishi Electronics America, Inc.
Cypress, CA 90630

Murata Business Systems, Inc.
4801 Spring Valley Road
Building 108B
Dallas, TX 75244
(214)392-1622

NEC America, Inc.
8 Old Sod Farm Road
Melville, NY 11747
(800)222-4632

Nissei Electric USA, Inc.
3 Reuten Drive
Closter, NJ 07624

Nitsuko
4 Forest Parkway
Shelton, CT 06484
(203)929-8407

Omnifax
Telautograph Corporation
8700 Bellanca Avenue
Los Angeles, CA 90045
(800)221-8330

Panafax
Panafax Corporation
10 Melville Park Road
Melville, NY 11747
(800)645-7486

Panasonic
Data Communication Products
One Panasonic Way
Secaucus, NJ 07094
(201)348-9090

Pitney Bowes Facsimile
Stamford, CT 06926-0700
(800)672-6937

Radio Shack
A Division of Tandy Corporation
1700 One Tandy Center
Fort Worth, TX 76102

Ricoh Corporation
5 Dedrick Place
West Caldwell, NJ 07006
(800)524-0864

Sanyo Business Systems, Inc.
51 Joseph Street
Moonachie, NJ 07074
(201)440-9300

Savin Corporation
West Broad Street
Stamford, CT 06904-2270

Sharp Electronics Corporation
Sharp Plaza
Mahwah, NJ 07430
(201)529-8200

TIE/Communications, Inc.
8 Progress Drive
Shelton, CT 06484

Toshiba America, Inc.
Facsimile Products Group
9740 Irvine Boulevard
Irvine, CA 92718
(800)635-1220

Trans-Lux
110 Richards Avenue
Norwalk, CT 06854
(800)268-0491

Xerox Corporation
P.O. Box 24
Rochester, NY 14692
(800)832-6979

FAX MODEM AND FAX-RELATED SOFTWARE MANUFACTURERS

Fax modems and related software are quickly catching on in the fax marketplace. Using a fax modem eliminates the need to print out a document prior to faxing. In some cases, what you see on the screen is what the receiving fax-modem-equipped PC or Macintosh receives.

In addition to the fax modem, computer software manufacturers have developed sophisticated, easy-to-use software packages that increase the utility of these devices. Several manufacturers have developed software that turns a fax machine into a powerful scanner that can read text and graphic materials and place them onto the computer's screen where they can be edited and used with programs such as desktop publishing.

PC-Fax Modem Manufacturers

Advanced Vision Research
1943 Hartog Drive
San Jose, CA 95131
(408)434-1115

American Data Technology, Inc.
44 West Bellevue Drive
Pasadena, CA 91105
(818)578-1339

Asher Technologies, Inc.
1009-I Mansell Road
Roswell, GA 30076
(404)993-4590

Brooktrout Technology, Inc.
110 Cedar Street
Wellesley Hills, MA 02181
(617)235-3026

Carterfone
Communications Corporation
1341 W. Mockingbird Lane
Dallas, TX 75247
(214)634-2424

Complete PC, The
521 Cottonwood Drive
Milpitas, CA 95035
(408)434-0145

Datacopy Corporation
1215 Terra Bella Avenue
Mountain View, CA 94043
(415)965-7900

Dest Corporation
1201 Cadillac Court
Milpitas, CA 95035
(408)946-7100

Electronic Information Technology, Inc.
25 Just Road
Fairfield, NJ 07006
(201)227-1447

Fax Partner
Panasonic Industrial Company
Division of Matsushita Electric Corporation of America
Two Panasonic Way
Secaucus, NJ 07094
(201)348-7000

GammaFax
GammaLink
2452 Embarcadero Way
Palo Alto, CA 94303
(415)856-7421

Gulfstream Micro Systems, Inc.
1065 S. Rogers Circle
Boca Raton, FL 33431
(800)443-0500

ImageCard
Ricoh Corporation
Communications Products Group
5 Dedrick Place
West Caldwell, NJ 07006
(201)882-2000

JT Fax
Quadram
One Quad Way
Norcross, GA 30093
(404)923-6666

MFAX96
Microtek Lab
16901 S. Western Ave.
Gardena, CA 90247
(213)321-2121

OAZ Communications, Inc.
15032 Redhill Ave.
Tustin, CA 92680
(714)259-0909

PC-Fax
E.I.T., Inc.
25 Just Road
Fairfield, NJ 07006
(201)227-1447

Pitney Bowes
Walter H. Wheeler Jr. Drive
Stamford, CT 06926
(203)882-2000

Rockwell International Corporation
Semiconductor Products Division
4311 Jamboree Road
Newport Beach, CA 92660
(714)883-6849

Spectrafax
2000 Palm Street
Naples, FL 33962
(813)775-2737

PC and PC Compatible Fax-Related Software

Read-IT! (Optical Character Recognition)
Olduvai Corporation
7520 Red Road
Suite A
South Miami, FL 33143
(305)665-4665
Fax (305)665-0671

Why waste time typing when, with Read-It! OCR software, you can turn your PC into a sophisticated optical character recognition system. Whether it's a massive database on paper, a manuscript, or a book—in fact almost any printed word, even in multiple columns—if your scanner can scan it, Read-It! OCR can turn it into usable text for your word processing or database application. With Read IT! OCR, you can scan a document and load it into your computer for editing, layout, etc. and then fax the finished document via a fax modem or print out the document for faxing via a stand-alone fax machine.

Macintosh Fax Modems and Fax-Related Software

The Apple Macintosh is an ideal candidate for creating an image communications workstation. The Mac's incredible graphics capabilities are particularly suited for fax communications because fax machines can print both text and graphics. Several manufacturers (besides Apple) offer fax modems. In addition, a number of software manufacturers offer software that operates with various fax modems.

MODEMS

AppleFax Modem
Apple Computer, Inc.
Cupertino, CA 95104

InterFax
Abaton
48431 Milmont Drive
Fremont, CA 94538
(415)683-3601

LightFax
Computer Friends
14250 NW Science Park Drive
Portland, OR 97229

MacFax Modem
Orchid Technology
45365 Northport Loop West
Fremont, CA 94538
(415)683-0300

The MacFax puts a high-speed data modem at your fingertips while turning a Macintosh into a powerful fax machine. Whether transferring Macintosh files or sending and receiving a fax, the MacFax will do so at a rate up to 9,600 bps.

MacFax can send and receive facsimiles from any Group II or Group III fax, connecting the user to virtually any installed fax machine around the world. Data communications are equally fast because MacFax is a full 9,600 bps data modem.

TransFax
Genius, Inc.
3958 Van Noord Avenue
Studio City, CA 91604
(818)905-8866

TransFax contains an eight-page buffer that can receive faxes while unattended, even when it's not attached to a Mac or if the Mac is turned off. An accompanying software package sends faxed files to the Mac once the computer is turned on.

SOFTWARE

BackFAX
Solutions International
30 Commerce Street
Williston, VT 05495
(802)658-5506

BackFAX is a fax communications software for the Macintosh and AppleFax modem that operates in the background. It can send or receive fax documents while another application is running, even without MultiFinder. It provides an easy way to send Mac documents directly to any Group III fax machine or computer with a fax modem—without giving up the use of the computer. It can also copy parts of documents received via the AppleFax modem for pasting into other Mac applications. BackFAX provides an intelligent address book to save frequently used fax numbers with delivery instructions, and it can operate automatically to delay sending fax documents until a later time.

Read-IT! (Optical Character Recognition)
Olduvai Corporation
7520 Red Road
Suite A
South Miami, FL 33143
(305)665-4665
Fax (305)665-0671

Read-It! OCR works with any scanner, reads TIFF, PICT, and Bitmap files, and also accepts drivers for direct scanner operation of most popular scanners.

Read-It! also works with fax modems, and if the Macintosh is running under MultiFinder, the user can be working in one application while Read-It! OCR is quietly going about its business in the background.

Since the program creates standard text files, the files can be used with any word-processing, database, spreadsheet or desktop publishing application. The user can edit, spell check, mail merge, change fonts and styles, or even perform calculations. The document is in the Macintosh with the user hardly lifting a finger.

With Read IT! OCR, you can scan a document and load it into your computer for editing, layout, etc., and then fax the finished document via a fax modem or print it out for faxing via a stand-alone fax machine.

SmartForm Series
Claris Corporation
440 Clyde Avenue
Mountain View, CA 94043

SmartForm Designer and SmartForm Assistant represent the start of a newly developing market in personal computer software—one in which Claris has made a long-term commitment. Electronic forms processing (EFP) is part of Claris' broader office products strategy that will revolve around tightly integrated communications and database capabilities.

SmartForm Designer allows Macintosh users to quickly create professional-looking forms for their personal use or for distribution within an organization. It is useful for simple forms as it is for complex ones and can be applied to any forms important in business, including expense reports, invoices, and sales receipts.

Forms created using SmartForm Designer can be printed and filled out manually or with a typewriter or they can be completed electronically on a Macintosh with SmartForm Assistant.

The SmartForm Series is ideally suited to the fax user and the rapid communications fax makes possible. Good-looking, effective forms are easily customized to meet individual business needs. Electronic forms processing represents a new category of personal computer software, but the needs served are integral to a broad range of business transactions.

Coupled with the use of a Macintosh and fax modem or a stand-alone fax machine, SmartForms makes sense out of the information every business needs to know. Likewise, Smartforms enables the user to create forms that help get the message across.

SCANNERS

Although most fax modems and their software provide a way to communicate with virtually any fax machine or similarly equipped computer, a scanner is sometimes required to input text and graphics. A scanner enables the user to input graphics and text into the computer's memory for editing. There are many different scanners available for both IBM, IBM compatibles, and Apple Macintosh computers. The following scanners, offered by Thunderware and Computer Friends, provide an affordable alternative to a desktop scanner.

Computer Friends

Computer Friends offers the LightScan hand-held scanner for Macintosh. This is a lightweight unit that allows for easy scanning of both text and graphics material.

Computer Friends
14250 NW Science Park Drive
Portland, OR 97229

Thunderware

LightningScan is a hand-held, high-resolution image scanner for the Macintosh. Its design allows fast scanning of photographs, images from books and magazines, drawings, and logos. Its speed and flexibility make it an ideal tool for all Macintosh graphics applications including desktop publishing and design. After use, the small scanning unit is easily stored in any desk drawer.

ThunderScan is an economical yet powerful scanner for just about the entire Apple computer line. The ThunderScan replaces the ribbon cartridge of any ImageWriter printer. Images to be scanned are rolled into the printer. The scanner zips back and forth, digitizing the image in 16 levels of gray. Its innovative design makes high-resolution scanning affordable. ThunderScan images can be edited and saved via its user-friendly software to be used in other programs.

Thunderware's scanners give added flexibility to computers and enhance image communications by providing an easy and affordable method of inputting text (when used with programs such as Olduvai's Read IT!) and graphics into the computer for editing, printing, and faxing.

Thunderware, Inc.
21 Orinda Way
Orinda, CA 94563
(415)254-3047

Appendix B

Fax Supplies, Publications, Services and Associations

THE GROWTH IN FAX MACHINE SALES AND USE HAS NOT STOPPED with the machines themselves. Riding high on the wave of the fax invasion of homes and offices are a host of suppliers offering fax papers, accessories, services, etc.

This appendix offers a listing of suppliers, services, and organizations. Check both yellow and white pages of your local telephone directories, as well as local business organizations such as Chamber of Commerce, for additional information on fax bureaus, etc.

ACCESSORIES AND SUPPLIES

Most office supply companies and catalogs offer supplies for the fax user. Fax accessories range from surge suppressors to telephone wall plates, jacks, plugs, and adapters to specially designed fax cabinets.

AccuFax Imaging Supplies
Paper Manufacturers Company
24 Triangle Park Drive
Cincinnati, OH 45246
(800)327-4359
In Ohio (800)423-8512
Fax (513)772-5098

Company offers a full line of thermal papers and imaging supplies including hard-to-find, high-sensitivity papers for the gray scale and shading capabilities of modern fax machines.

CPS Electronics L.C.
4151 112th Terrace North
P.O. Box 2460
Pinellas Park, FL 34664-2460
(800)572-6010
Fax (813)572-0589

Company offers accessories that provide protection from transient voltage surge on the hot, neutral, and ground lines of the telephone wires. CPS also offers a unit that plugs into a standard electrical receptacle (5-15R) and provides transient surge protection to two outlets.

Curtis Manufacturing Company
30 Fitzgerald Drive
Jaffrey, NH 03452
(603)532-4123

Curtis specializes in computer and fax accessories, especially accessories that protect equipment from voltage spikes and surges.

Demco, Inc.
4810 Forest Run Road
Box 7488
Madison, WI 53707
(608)241-1201
Fax (608)241-1799

Known for their wide range of office supplies, Demco offers attractive and functional fax stands with plenty of room for storing fax paper and other office supplies. Demco is a convenient source for fax machine papers because they do not require customers to buy in carton quantities. Buy just what you need, one or two rolls at a time.

Electronic Speech Systems, Inc.
1900 Powell Street, Suite 205
Emeryville, CA 94608
(415)547-2755

The company's FAX/Phone Switch II makes it possible for a phone and fax machine to share a single telephone line. The unit can distinguish between voice and fax (data) signals and switch calls to a telephone, fax, or modem.

Fax Care Company
100 Wilmont Road #347
Deerfield, IL 60015
Company manufactures the Fax Care cleaning kit for fax machines.

Murata Business Systems, Inc.
4801 Spring Valley Road
Building 108B
Dallas, TX 75244
(214)392-1622
Besides fax machines, Murata offers the Faxcessory assortment of fax care products.

ONEAC Corporation
27944 North Bradley Road
Libertyville, IL 60048
(800)533-7166

Panamax
150 Mitchell Boulevard
San Rafael, CA 94903-2057
(800)472-5555

Radio Shack
A Division of Tandy Corporation
1700 One Tandy Center
Fort Worth, TX 76102
Known for their electronic components, Radio Shack is a kind of one-stop accessory center. If you need to extend the reach of a telephone line, add a telephone jack, or add a telephone extension cord, Radio Shack should be the first stop.

3M Company
Box 33600
St. Paul, MN 55133-3600
3M offers Post-It Fax transmittal memo notes that attach to a corner of transmitted documents. Notes provide space for informa-

tion usually included on transmittal cover sheets and are printed with black ink on white paper for enhanced facsimile reproduction. Each pad contains 50 1.5-by-4-inch notes.

PUBLICATIONS

The following publications regularly feature information on fax machines and accessories.

Geyer's Office Dealer
51 Madison Avenue
New York, NY 10010
(212)689-4411

Modern Office Technology
1100 Superior Avenue
Cleveland, OH 44114
(216)696-7000

Office Products Bulletin
1805 Underwood Boulevard
Delran, NJ 08075
(800)328-2776

The Office
1600 Summer Street
Stamford, CT 06430
(203)255-4100

Spec Check Facsimile Guide
($60/year)
Dataquest
1290 Ridder Park Drive
San Jose, CA 95131-2398
(800)624-3282
In California (408)971-9661
This publication, published twice yearly, has complete specifications for all makes and models of facsimile machines. It does not include test reports.

What to Buy for Business
($135/year; $30 single issue)

What to Buy, Inc.
350 Theodore Fremd Avenue
Rye, NY 10580
(800)247-2185

ELECTRONIC REFERENCE PRODUCTS

Franklin Computer Corporation offers an entire line of electronic reference products that combine the authority and familiarity of books with the speed, ease, and fun of electronics. Franklin's compact and authoritative electronic library offers reference tools for spelling, reading, and writing—spelling correctors, thesauruses, and dictionaries.

Franklin's line of more than a dozen comprehensive, accurate and authoritative products can help ensure that fax communications are written more clearly, effectively, and accurately. From desktop to pocket-size models, each Franklin product features a built-in, high-quality database of American English words from Merriam-Webster's dictionary.

Franklin Computer Corporation
122 Burrs Road
Mt. Holly, NJ 08060
(609)261-4800

FAX DIRECTORIES

The following directories offer listings of fax users and listings of fax machines that are available in libraries.

The Directory of Telefacsimile Sites in Libraries in the United States and Canada
($18)
CBR Consulting Services
Box 248
Buchanan Dam, TX 78609-0248
(512)793-6118

Facsimile Users' Directory
Monitor Publishing Company
104 Fifth Avenue
2nd Floor
New York, NY 10011
(212)627-4140

This company publishes other directories such as *The Congressional Yellow Book.*

The FAX Directory
Enterpreneurs' Library
P.O. Box 17509
Fountain Hills, AZ 85269-7509

FAX Phone Book
Dial-A-Fax Directories Corporation
1761 W. Hillsboro Boulevard
Deerfield Beach, FL 33442
(800)346-3329

The Official Facsimile Users' Directory
FDP Associates
One Park Avenue
New York, NY 10016
(212)530-4100

SUBSCRIPTION SERVICES

The following subscription services and long-distance telephone carriers offer services that enable computer owners and fax owners to communicate more conveniently. Dramatic reduction in technology costs and greater competition have reduced the cost of sending messages via the computer or E-mail (electronic mail).

Fax-to-fax services have also joined in the market and offer users reduced phone rates by charging flat rates for thirty seconds and then charging in six-second increments for fax calls, toll-free numbers, and credit cards and account numbers that give mobility to frequent fax users (no longer tied to one machine). The big advantage to using fax-to-fax services is their ability to handle busy retries, use of store-and-forward technology, and their broadcasting features that make multiple deliveries a snap.

AT&T MailFAX
(800)367-7225

Available to AT&T Mail subscribers, AT&T MailFAX delivers electronic text to any fax machine using Group III transmission standards. Fax machines do not have to be registered with AT&T Mail to receive messages. A user can send a single message to multiple fax machines at the same time. Fax deliveries can even be mixed with other delivery options such as electronic, U.S. Mail, and overnight delivery of hard copy.

EasyPlex-Fax Link
CompuServe Information Service
Dept. L Box 477
P.O. Box 18161
Columbus, OH 43272-4630
(800)848-8199

Membership to CompuServe is required. EasyPlex-Fax Link allows users to send messages to facsimile machines worldwide without having to own a fax machine or adding a fax board to their computer. The system is easy to use: compose a text message—be it a letter, contract, sales report, investment document, etc. or any text document that has been composed using a personal computer. EasyPlex-Fax Link sends the document to the telephone number(s) the user indicates and informs the sender when the message is transmitted.

MCI Mail
1150 17th Street, NW
Suite 800
Washington, D.C. 20036
(800)444-6245

MCI Mail's FaxDispatch lets users send messages from their terminals to fax machines located worldwide. If necessary, MCI Mail will automatically make several attempts to deliver messages to busy phone numbers.

Telenet Fax
A US Sprint Company
12490 Sunrise Valley Drive
Reston, VA 22096
(800)835-3638

Telenet Fax lets customers send ASCII messages directly from their terminal, personal computer, or private electronic mail service to any Group III fax machine.

EasyLink FAX
Western Union Corporation
One Lake Street
Upper Saddle River, NJ 07458
(800)247-1373

EasyLink FAX enables users to compose messages on their computer's screen and send it to EasyLink instead of feeding page after page through a fax machine, redialing busy numbers. If requested, the sender receives delivery confirmation.

FAX SERVICES

Now popping up in hotels, airports, and train stations, self-service fax machines and fax service bureaus enable nonfax owners to take advantage of fax technology without the cost of purchasing a machine. Most fax service centers charge a flat rate per page plus telephone connect charges.

AT&T FAX FIRST
AT&T
(Check with a local AT&T Phone Center for details.)

AT&T's FAX FIRST lets customers send and receive facsimile copies of printed material between any two AT&T Phone Centers or between a Phone Center and any compatible facsimile machine in the world.

Customers use the service by taking the pages they want to send to a Phone Center where a representative transmits them on an AT&T facsimile machine. If the fax is sent to another Phone Center, a representative at the receiving end will notify the recipient by phone that a fax message can be picked up at the store. There is no charge for the page identifying the sender and recipient.

CREDIT CARD FAX

Faxit Corporation
Cherry Hill, NJ

Faxit Corporation offers the world's first commercial credit-card-activated public facsimile system. The system has been installed at major U.S. airports where travelers can use a major credit card to charge fax service fees.

ASSOCIATIONS

American Facsimile Association
1701 Arch Street
Philadelphia, PA 19103
(215)568-8336

International Fax Association
4023 Lakeview Drive
Lake Havasu City, AZ 86403
(602)453-3850

National Office Machine Dealers Association (NOMDA)
12411 Wornall Road
Kansas City, MO 64145
(816)941-3100

Glossary

3/2/1 compatibility—Compatibility with earlier Group I and Group II fax units enables Group III machines to exchange information with virtually all makes and models of telefax equipment in use. (See *automatic step-down*.)

acoustic coupler—An attachment used with portable fax machines to communicate via nonmodular telephones, such as hard-wired hotel phones.

activity log—provides a chronological record of send and receive operations.

adjustable gray scale—Permits gray-scale adjustments for more faithful reproduction of graphic material such as photographs and drawings. This feature is particularly useful where transmissions frequently involve graphic material. This feature must be used carefully; it increases transmission time dramatically. In addition, improper gray scale can produce good graphics but render poor text quality.

automatic answer/disconnect—The fax machine can receive transmissions unattended. The unit answers the phone, receives the facsimile, disconnects, and awaits other calls. Some machines include a built-in telephone answering machine and can answer as either a fax machine or telephone answering machine.

automatic dialing—Frequently called fax telephone numbers can be entered and stored in the memory of the fax machine and dialed at the push of a button. This feature eliminates the need for rekeying phone numbers (especially useful when the line is busy) and reduces chances of dialing errors.

automatic document feeder—Enables a machine to send multipage documents unattended and works in conjunction with automatic dialing capabilities to permit fully automatic operation. There are two basic types of document feeders—top and bottom feed. Top feeders use gravity as they insert pages from a bin which rests at an angle atop the machine. Bottom feeders rely on a bin-and-roller-type mechanism to guide sheets into the machine. Most machines capable of feeding more than five sheets of paper use a top-feeding system.

automatic paper cutter—Enables the machine to automatically cut each incoming document to the length of the original and allows receipt of numerous consecutive messages and multipage documents without having to cut each page apart manually.

automatic reception—Sets up the fax to receive documents unattended.

automatic redial—When machines with this feature reach a busy signal, they can redial the busy number up to 15 times at 15-minute intervals.

automatic reduction—Fax units equipped with this feature can automatically reduce oversized incoming documents to fit the paper available for printing. This feature generally affects only the width of the document because length is limited only by the length of the paper roll within the printing fax.

automatic send and receive—This feature enables a fax machine to automatically dial and send documents. Such machines require automatic document feed, delayed dialing, and automatic disconnect features. Auto receive enables a machine to automatically answer the phone, receive incoming fax transmissions, and disconnect at the conclusion of the transmission.

automatic step-down—Most Group III fax machines transmit at 9,600 bits per second (bps), under ideal conditions. When poor phone line conditions (noise, static, etc.) won't allow faster transmission speeds or when communicating with earlier generation fax units (Group I or II machines), the machine slows down transmission speed as necessary, increasing transmission time from as little as 19 seconds per page up to three minutes or longer.

automatic transmission—Allows user to send a multipaged document without feeding each page manually. (See *automatic send/receive*.)

baud—A unit of communications processing speed in telegraphy and digital data communications systems, usually equal to a rate of one bit per second.

broadcasting—Documents are transmitted simultaneously to a number of other facsimile systems. This is especially useful when a document needs to be sent to a number of locations at the same time.

CCITT—Consultative Committee for International Telephone and Telegraphy.

coded dialing—Complements the one-touch (see *one-touch*) feature by enabling user to store phone numbers in the fax machine's memory and access them by pressing a two-digit abbreviated phone number. Use one-touch for frequently dialed numbers and coded dialing for numbers used less often. Some machines can store more than 100 numbers.

confidentiality—Enables a fax machine to receive a transmission without printing it out. Instead, the document is retained in memory until a security code is entered, then the document is printed.

contrast/document enhancement—Helps maintain the legibility of documents with dark-colored backgrounds and permits the user to increase the sharpness of poor originals. Some machines allow manual adjustment as opposed to automatic mode. Settings vary from light, normal, to dark contrast, similar to photocopy machines.

copier—This feature enables a fax machine to double as a photocopier.

date and time stamp—Incoming documents are automatically marked with date, time, and identifier of the transmitting fax unit.

delayed dialing—Enables a fax machine to send items loaded into the document feeder or stored in memory during off-peak hours when phone rates are lower. Most units equipped with this feature can send delayed messages to more than a dozen locations. (See *broadcast.*)

diagnostics—Checks the functions of the fax machine and produces a printed report upon completion of the test. Some manufacturers offer dial-up diagnostic capabilities to check a machine over the phone lines.

distribution lists—Fax numbers of recipients on a distribution list programmed into the machine's memory. The unit can then automatically transmit to recipients without the user keying in the telephone numbers.

document identification—Incoming documents are automatically identified with a date-and-time stamp and the identification number of the transmitting fax unit. Users with deadlines to meet can verify the exact time and date of incoming facsimile documents.

dot-matrix printer—A computer output peripheral that prints characters as a matrix of dots using a number of styli; a common character matrix is 5 X 7, i.e., 35 dots.

ECM (error correction mode)—Causes the fax machine to automatically resend data if line noise has garbled the transmission. This feature helps ensure that what you sent was received.

editing—Permits deletion of unneeded portion of a document prior to sending.

effective print width—The maximum width on which the fax can print incoming documents.

effective scanning width—The maximum width of document content that the machine can read and transmit. A wider scanning width minimizes the likelihood of losing part of the text at the margin area.

facsimile—A process or the result of a process by which fixed graphic material including text, photographs, or images is scanned and the information converted into electrical signal waves that are used either locally or remotely to produce in recorded form a likeness (facsimile) of the subject copy.

facsimile receiver—The complete device or system that selects, amplifies, and demodulates a picture signal picked up from the air, wires, or cables and employs the elements of this signal to reproduce the picture.

facsimile recorder—The machine that puts a transmitted facsimile image on paper.

facsimile signal—The signal resulting from the scanning in a facsimile system.

facsimile signal level—An expression of the maximum signal power or voltage created by the scanning of the subject copy, as measured at any given point in a facsimile system. Depending on whether the system employs positive or negative modulation, this will correspond to picture white or black, respectively. Signal level can be expressed in decibels with respect to a standard value, such as 1 milliwatt or 1 volt.

facsimile system—An integrated assembly of the elements used for facsimile transmission and reception.

facsimile transmission—The transmission of signal waves produced by the scanning process.

facsimile transmitter—The complete device or system that generates signals depicting graphic material (pictures, writing, printing, etc.) and sends them to a distant point—via cable, wire lines, or radio—for subsequent reproduction.

fallback—A condition in processing when special computer or manual functions must be employed as either complete or partial substitutes for malfunctioning systems. Such procedures could be used anywhere between complete system availability and total system failure. Fax machines will fall back from a higher transmission speed to a slower speed when the connection is poor or when the machine is unable to connect at a higher speed.

fallback procedure—A procedure to circumvent all equipment faults. The fallback could give degraded service and might include switching to an alternate computer or to different output devices and so on.

fallback recovery—The restoration of a system to full operation from a fallback mode of operation after the cause of the fallback has been removed.

fax phone—A fax machine combined with a telephone forming a compact desktop unit.

gray scale—Shades of gray used by a fax machine to more faithfully reproduce photographs and graphics. Most fax transmissions (text) are black and white. (See adjustable gray scale.)

Group I—Early fax units with transmission rates of four to six minutes per page.

Group II—Fax machines developed in the United States in the mid seventies by Graphic Sciences (since absorbed by Fujitsu) and 3M. Group II fax units transmit at a rate of approximately three minutes per page.

Group III—Current-generation fax machines developed during the seventies by the Japanese. Although digital themselves, Group III machines can automatically switch to an analog mode for communication with Group I or Group II fax units. Group III machines commonly transmit at a speed of 9,600 bps (bits per second) or from 9 to 20 seconds per page with resolution up to 200 X 200 dpi (dots per inch).

Group IV—Next-generation fax machines offering higher resolution at nearly twice the current transmission speeds. Group IV machines can transmit at speeds up to 56 kbps (kilobits per second) or about five seconds per page with resolution up to 400 X 400 dpi (dots per inch). Because these units use digital transmission, they require the use of digital circuits and satellite networks; access to such lines is very expensive and is not presently widely available.

Group IV upgrade—Offered by some manufacturers, this allows owners of Group III units to upgrade to Group IV machines.

group dial—Telephone numbers assigned to a group of fax machines. When preprogrammed codes are pressed, documents are sent to each machine in that group.

halftone—Standard fax transmission sends photographs in black and white. Halftone provides up to 32 shades of gray. Halftone provides more faithful reproduction of the original document, which is especially good for transmitting photographs.

laser printer—Unlike thermal printers, a laser printer utilizes laser technology to provide resolution of about 400 X 400 dots per inch. This allows for high-quality reproduction of photographs and graphics.

local ID—The ID number (normally the telephone number) of the fax machine.

management audit report—Provides a record of transactions (receiving location, transmission length, number of pages, and incomplete transmissions). Useful for client charge-backs. Some fax units imprint incoming documents with the originating fax unit's location and phone number, some can confirm whether or not a transmission was successfully sent and received, others include the date, time, and duration of each transmission.

manual receive—Permits the fax operator to answer the telephone for voice communication.

maximum original size—The size of the largest original the fax can accommodate. Width is the important factor, length generally is limited by the length of the paper roll in the machine.

memory—Enables a fax machine to store information such as time/date, telephone numbers, and confidential or security transmissions for later printout.

modem—A device that converts data from a form that is compatible with data-processing equipment (computers) to a form that is compatible with transmission facilities (phone lines, etc.) and vice versa.

one-touch dialing—Allows user to store frequently used phone numbers in the machine's memory and transmit to those locations by loading the document and pressing a single button.

oversized documents—Larger documents, such as computer printouts, which are automatically reduced by the sending fax before transmission.

PC-fax interface—Installation of a special computer board and software enables a PC user to display text and graphics received via facsimile and manipulate the data and store it on disk. The PC user can also transmit to facsimile machines via the fax computer board or interface.

plain-paper fax—Unlike the thermal paper fax unit, which transfers an image directly from a metal surface to thermal sensitive paper, plain-paper fax units use a carbonlike ribbon to transfer images from a heated surface onto sheets of paper. Plain paper fax copies will not fade.

polling—Programming a fax unit to automatically dial other units at predetermined times to receive messages awaiting transmission.

portable fax—Weighing under ten pounds, these units can be taken on trips and used from most telephones (see acoustic coupler), including cellular car phones.

programmable phone—Allows the user to store long sequences of telephone numbers in memory for access with a single keystroke. Most units allow the user to program pauses in dialing needed for access to phone networks (outside lines) or long-distance phone service.

ready tones—Continuous series of tones with a pause between each series.

remote security ID—The ID number of a selected remote machine that is authorized to poll another fax machine.

resolution—The degree to which closely adjacent parts of an image can be differentiated.

roll size—Size of roll of paper used by the fax machine. Some units accept paper rolls 150 feet long, others 300 feet long. Width can vary from 8.5 up to 11 inches wide.

RS232-C interface—Enables use of fax machine as a computer output printer or as a scanner for inputting documents into a personal computer, provided compatible software is used.

security—A feature found on many units that permits the transmission of confidential information through the use of assigned security codes. Instead of printing information as it is received, it is stored in memory and printed only when a security code is entered into the machine.

send confirm—A brief report for the send operator confirming the successful transmission of all pages sent.

sender header print—A one-line message printed at the top of the received document containing the sender's name, date, time, phone number, and the page number.

sending speed—See *transmission speed.*

speed dialing—Permits the programming of frequently called fax telephone numbers.

store and forward—Documents are stored in the fax unit's memory and transmitted later, usually when phone rates are lowest.

system controller—Similar to the devices used with photocopying machines, these can identify each person and/or department using the facsimile system and generate management reports. This can be useful if departments are to be billed (charge-back) for their fax usage.

teleconferencing—A combination of speakerphone, transparency printer and fax unit for simultaneous transmission of voice and graphics to teleconference participants. This feature is useful when charts and graphic materials are discussed.

thermal paper—Special chemically treated, thermal-sensitive paper used in most fax machines. Incoming electrical signals are converted to heat variations on a metal surface. The thermal paper reproduces the original image when it comes in contact with the metal.

throughput, simultaneous—Where a computer is functioning at the same time that input and output data is being transferred.

time delay—Document can be placed in machine and broadcast, unattended, at a later time.

transducer—A device that converts one quantity into another quantity, specifically when one of the quantities is electrical. Thus, a loudspeaker converts electrical impulses into sound, a microphone converts sound into electrical impulses, a photocell converts light into electricity, a thermocouple converts heat into electricity, and so on.

transfer—Permits transmission of data to a single station in a distant city where it is transmitted to several other stations in the same city.

transfer rate—The rate at which a transfer of data between the computer's memory and storage, input, or output devices occurs. It is usually expressed as a number of characters per second.

transmission accounting—A record-keeping feature that tracks the number and length of messages transmitted and their destinations.

transmission speed—The time it takes a fax unit to transmit a page, expressed as pages per minute. Typical transmission rates generally do not reflect the time it takes for two fax machines to establish a communications link. This "handshake" period lasts about fifteen seconds.

user options log—Provides the operator with a status of all the special programmable options that are input in the set state.

voice ID—Allows a user to record a personal message so that when his or her fax machine is called, the sender hears a verbal confirmation that the right machine has been reached.

voice request—Allows the user to fax an item and then talk with someone at the receiving fax unit on the same call without having to place an additional phone call (a phone handset is required).

Index